GW00381718

GARDENING WITHOUT CHEMICALS

A Step-by-Step Guide to Growing
Vegetables and Soft Fruit the
Organic Way.

Here's Health Guide to

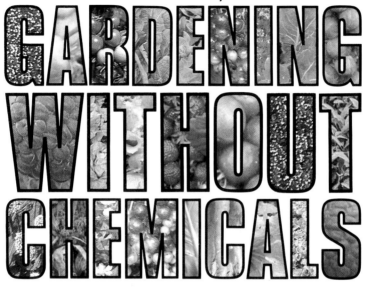

GARDENING WITHOUT CHEMICALS

*A Step-by-Step Guide
to Growing Vegetables and
Soft Fruit the Organic Way*

by

Jack Temple

THORSONS PUBLISHING GROUP
Wellingborough · New York

First published 1986

© THORSONS PUBLISHING GROUP 1986

All rights reserved. No part of this book may be reproduced or utilized in any form or by any means, electronic or mechanical, including photocopying, recording or by any information storage and retrieval system, without permission in writing from the Publisher.

British Library Cataloguing in Publication Data

Temple, Jack
   Gardening without chemicals.
   1. Organic gardening
   I. Title
   635'.0484   SB453.5

   ISBN 0-7225-1135-3

Printed in Italy

Contents

Foreword

Organic gardening means different things to different people and, as yet, there is no really satisfactory definition or indeed any 'official' explanation of what the term means. One approach is to regard organic gardening as an attempt to grow plants, mainly for food, in as natural an environment as possible, without recourse to artificial agents for destroying pests and to fertilizers that are not balanced with reference to their mineral ingredients. Organic gardeners tend to avoid chemical pesticides and the reason is not hard to find. Any agent that destroys life in the form of insects and harmful micro-organisms must also attack the human body to varying degrees. No destructive agent has yet been invented that will not in some way induce harmful effects in animals and man. The route into the body of these agents is mainly via the food — precautions can be taken by the grower whilst applying these chemicals but there is little control of their uptake by plants. Many of these substances, by their very nature, are fat-soluble which means that, once they are introduced into the body, they accumulate in the fatty tissues where they remain for very long periods. Little is known about the long-term effects of such residues.

This, then, is the negative approach to organic gardening in the sense that potentially toxic chemicals are avoided and control of garden pests, of all varieties, is left to natural methods that are effective and harmless. These methods, often involving simultaneously growing adjacent plants that have a protective action, or controlling the soil environment to discourage insects, are described in this book and are worthy of attention. It is on the positive approach, however, that the book has particular value, because the provision of organic nutrients in the form of naturally-produced fertilizers is the very basis of organic gardening.

Minerals needed by growing plants are supplied in the air and in the soil. Photosynthesis allows some nutrients to be produced from atmospheric carbon dioxide and the nitrogen in the air is 'fixed' by specific micro-organisms that live in the soil. Everything else the plants need is supplied from the soil itself and, if these are provided, the plant is capable of producing all its own requirements of nutrients. In this respect, plants are far more efficient than animals because the latter must have some micro-nutrients, such as vitamins, as part of the diet since they are incapable of manufacturing their own. Plants make their own vitamins, for their own use, from the minerals supplied in the soil and the gases, carbon dioxide and nitrogen, provided in the air. Hence, in the presence of ample air, the limiting factors for the healthy growth of any plant are the minerals in the soil. If one or more of these is absent or deficient, the growth and health of the plant will suffer.

The essential difference therefore between conventional and organic gardening lies in the provision of minerals to the plant, not only in their balance in terms of concentrations present, but in the manner in which they are presented to the plant. Organic fertilizers are composed not only of minerals presented in their organic or easily assimilable form but also of other matter that can improve the texture and water-retaining properties of the soil. None of these are provided in the conventional N-P-K (nitrogen, phosphorus and potassium) inorganic fertilizers that are widely used. The origins of organic fertilizers are rotted-down plants, seaweed, animal and bird excreta and even mulched paper and domestic waste, which together contain all the minerals needed by a plant presented in their correct balance.

Today, as our knowledge of soil and of plant metabolism increases, there is more awareness of the importance of the so-called trace minerals in ensuring healthy growth of plants. These minerals were largely ignored in the past because their presence was not known (precise analytical methods for their detection and measurement had not been developed) and even when known, their appearance in soil was often taken for granted. Now we know that such assumptions are not true, as some soils can lack these essential micronutrients. Organic fertilizers, because of the very nature of their origin, must contain all the minerals, trace and otherwise, needed for healthy growth. No man-made fertilizer, obtained by blending inorganic minerals dug from the ground, can do so.

The principles of organic gardening are presented in this book in a simple, easy-to-follow guide system that embodies all the good features of this approach to gardening. One example will illustrate just how important a balanced supply of all minerals in the soil is, not only to the plant but to those who eat it. Some regions of Poland were found to have a very high incidence of leukaemia and certain types of cancers, and careful investigation revealed a link between them and the soil of those areas. A fungus, called *Aspergillus flavus* was found to flourish in the soil and this particular micro-organism was known to be capable of producing cancer-inducing substances. The fact that it did flourish was a direct result of iron, copper and magnesium deficiencies in the soil, coupled with an excess of silicon and potassium. The latter was due to overfertilization of the area with conventional N-P-K fertilizers of the synthetic variety. Redressing the balance by supplying the deficient minerals controlled the fungus effectively and the incidence of cancer reduced dramatically.

This also serves to illustrate how everything in the soil, nutrients and poisons alike, finds its way into plants and eventually into those who eat the plants. How important, then, to ensure by the organic approach to gardening that the plants you are to eat are balanced in minerals (from a balanced soil), replete in vitamins and free from artificial additives. Only organic gardening can guarantee these desirable features.

LEN MERVYN

Introduction

I never actually set out in life to write a book. But I suppose it all started in 1940, really, when I was rejected by the armed forces. I was a medical reject. I had an unhappy history of poor personal health which started even before I was born. In the year 1917, England was blockaded. My mother was short of nutrition and so I was born with rickets, a pigeon chest and a jaw slightly out of place. A poor start by any standard. My mother placed my health in the hands of the medical profession to rectify glaring errors of physical deficiencies. The profession responded with all the care and all the know-how that they could muster. But their tools of the trade comprised of knife, medicants, drugs and vaccines, and by the time I was eighteen I had had enough. Seventeen operations for catarrh and other similar troubles and still more to come. I started to look for an alternative. The alternative in those days (and I am talking about the mid-thirties) was naturopathy, a method of healing the body by natural means, with methods used for hundreds of years which steered clear of knife, medicants and vaccines.

The man I consulted ignored my ailments, and my catarrh wasn't even discussed. It was what I was doing to myself that occupied most of the available time. The advice of the naturopath was the first glimmer that anybody had ever given me that health had something to do with me, that it certainly wasn't reliant on the man in the white coat. Good health was within my own grasp. He pointed out my need for a whole range of vitamins and minerals, but what he emphasized most was the need to eat whole foods grown on composted soils. A tall order for a young man working in the City of London.

Then fate intervened. A panel of seven doctors in 1940 decided that I was totally unfit for War Service and so, when an appeal was broadcast for increased food production, it fired my imagination. I decided I was to become a grower of organic foods. Thus growing became my profession for thirty-five years. Time enough for ample demonstrations of the close link between one's own personal health, linked with the health of the food consumed. This in turn was linked with the health of the soil which produced the food. Time enough for observation of what was happening all around to those who thought they needn't bother with Nature.

It was 1974 when I accepted the invitation to write on a regular basis in the popular health magazine *Here's Health*, on the subject of chemical-free organic gardening. I made no apology for the amount of space I devoted in my columns to pointing out how chemically-grown food is being devalued in vitamin and mineral content and, worse still, contains much in the way of harmful poisons.

Because of this, I set aside one acre of hungry, impoverished soil to prove that, even on the poorest soil and with no chemicals whatever, it is perfectly possible to build up to healthy fertility and disease-free crops. And by only writing about things I had already done myself I intended to scotch that hoary old myth that it is impossible to manage without chemicals. And if, by reading this book, it gives other people the means of regaining and retaining glowing health it will all have been worthwhile.

Part 1

Why choose organic gardening?

HEALTH and longevity are two things man has sought from time immemorial. When I came across the research carried out by Dr David Davis into the secrets of longevity some years ago, it made very exciting reading. Dr Davis had been a medical scientist at St Pancras Hospital in London, and he travelled the world visiting areas where peoples well-known for longevity lived off their own produce. His research concluded that there was a positive link between longevity and food grown in the way nature intended; in other words organically grown produce.

He realized that the quality of the soil was an important factor because, in each area he studied, his results were the same every time. The soil that supported peoples of longevity contained minerals which each time included chromium, calcium and iron.

Closer to home is the village of Upper Sheringham in Norfolk, where life expectancy has been put at ninety. The inhabitants grow their own food and the soil there contains chromium, calcium and iron. It is these valuable minerals which modern, Western forms of agriculture are so efficient at eliminating from our soil. What has shown up in work at agricultural and horticultural research stations is that all the chemicals so freely used in our modern growing techniques have caused imbalances in the soil. Vital minerals are either locked up by chemicals or lost to us. Whatever happens, they rarely, if ever, arrive as nourishment on our plates when chemical growing methods prevail.

The Rothampstead Research Station reported that after four years of chemically fertilized corn crops, copper disappeared from the soil completely. Consequently farmers have been obliged to introduce copper and other minerals into animal feeds.

This is the inescapable reason why the soil which grows our food must be chemical-free before the food that we grow can bring us the health we are entitled to.

1.   When choosing land for growing avoid poorly drained soil because, coupled with British weather, results will be poor.

2.   Large pools of surface water (background) are a warning sign of bad drainage and therefore poor crops.

3.   Wooden walls or frames allow the soil within beds to be raised to help drainage.

4.   Soil should be higher at the northern end of raised beds because a south-facing slope receives most light.

5.   Other plants can benefit from the shelter of the frame walls without being in the shade.

6.   Plants grown indoors in seed raisers can get on early in the garden when protected by sheets of perforated plastic. Perforated plastic allows plants to breathe and means early vegetables can be raised on exposed sites.

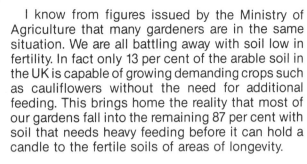

I know from figures issued by the Ministry of Agriculture that many gardeners are in the same situation. We are all battling away with soil low in fertility. In fact only 13 per cent of the arable soil in the UK is capable of growing demanding crops such as cauliflowers without the need for additional feeding. This brings home the reality that most of our gardens fall into the remaining 87 per cent with soil that needs heavy feeding before it can hold a candle to the fertile soils of areas of longevity.

How to start

ORGANIC gardening is simple. There is nothing mysterious about it and no reason to put people off. It means adding organic material and natural minerals to the soil, in order to bring it up to a level equal to areas of longevity which Dr Davis visited. As there are many ways to bring soil up to a high level of fertility, rich in minerals and humus, it allows everyone to join in, or begin organic gardening whether they have a large or small plot on which to grow food.

Choosing the right system to suit the amount of time available is very important. Organic gardening doesn't have to be complicated. During the time that it takes to produce your own well-rotted compost from raw materials there are products which can help to bring soil up to fertile levels. But organic gardening doesn't have to be expensive. For those who have more time and less money there are lots of materials that can be gathered at no cost.

More later on composting and bringing soil up to fertility.

There is also the aspect that by producing a healthy soil many of the problems suffered by those who grow their crops using artificial chemical fertilizers are obviated; such as the use of pesticides, herbicides and other chemicals. That is not to say that organic gardens are free from pests, but with healthier plants natural pest control methods are usually sufficient to combat any infestations.

7. Raised beds are formed by moving soil from the sides to make a long central raised ridge.

8. Raised beds can also be made to slope from north to south. Pipe is plumb to show slope of ground being made into bed.

9. Raised beds or frames can be covered with glass panels (behind frame) to turn cold, wet sites into early cropping areas.

10. Raised beds also allow for crops to be planted closer together because tall crops do not overshadow shorter ones.

11. Soil is removed to form drainage channel (centre) and placed on left to raise bed. Note different levels on which gardeners are standing.

12. View of the mature cropping area created by raised beds.

Choosing a garden

ONE of the most important points to bear in mind when gardening for health is the choice of situation. For example, many housing estates embrace gardens that slope acutely to the north. Results from such gardens will be disappointing. Spring growth will always be late and, added to this, the autumn growth will cease well before normal time. Even worse is a north-sloping garden which also has bad soil drainage. Such gardens can never supply a continuous amount of produce for a household, and they should be avoided at all costs.

Therefore the first thing to look for is a site that is well-drained. Soil type is not all that important because much can be done to improve fertility, but many times I have seen crops that do not progress because of inadequate drainage. British weather means such poor sites will need a lot of luck to thrive and produce good crops more than one year in five. This is not good enough for long-term investment.

I would advise would-be purchasers to seriously consider the drainage. March or November are the two best months for judging. Visit the site and take a spade because it is the water lurking just underneath the surface at a spade's depth which tells the story. A well-drained soil will never hold excess water.

Decisions should not be taken in haste. In a garden with a southern aspect, but with bad drainage, much can be done to improve the cropping area. For example most of my cropping beds have been raised from level and low-lying beds into higher beds with a higher northern side, sloping down to the south. A convenient ditch then takes away surplus water. I find this technique far superior to the conventional way of laying drainage pipes just under the surface in the hope that percolation will carry away surplus water.

Shelter is most important as well. Fences, trees, shrubs or artificial windbreaks will trap the warmth from the early spring sun. Good shelter will also break up the cold north or east winds which can retard growth for weeks on end. Permeable fences have been shown to be better than solid walls or fences in controlling winds and increasing temperatures. Winds have a nasty way of increasing speed when faced with solid walls, and once clear of the top of the wall they dive down in fiendish fashion in all their increased speed.

13.   Early summer cabbage and cauliflower enjoy double protection of V-trenches and perforated plastic covering.

14.   When plants are big enough, covering is removed, soil levelled and compost applied.

15.   The end result is a perfect brassica crop free from fly damage.

A garden aid which has become very popular in recent years is the covering of crops with permeable plastic sheets. I have used such sheets to forward garden crops with dramatic success. Furthermore, the covering of early-planted summer cabbage and cauliflower with these sheets controls the onslaught of root-fly attacks.

In fact, coaxing food crops from any soil which is less than perfect means adopting all sorts of special techniques. In the case of situations where there is no choice other than to make the best of unsuitable sites, my advice is simple. Grow as many crops as possible during the best growing months to provide a good surplus for freezing. From a health viewpoint I am convinced that frozen organic produce is superior in every way to fresh chemically grown produce.

Part 2

Feeding the soil

HAVING chosen the site for your organic garden the next job is to work on the soil to bring it up to a level of fertility that will produce plants full of health and vigour.

Two vital ingredients for healthy soil are humus and minerals. These are found in compost, but making compost is a slow process. Luckily there are now products available that are chemical-free and acceptable for use in the organic garden until the compost making process is well underway.

For example, Clavering Organics sell a very good product based on mushroom compost in their *Real* range. Working a good layer of this into the top few inches of any soil will work wonders in building up humus requirements for brassicas. Mineral requirements can be met by applying calcified seaweed at the same time. The rate of application will vary according to the quality of the soil, but an average rate ranges from 4-16oz (100-450g) to the square yard.

Vegetables growing in the surrounding area can provide a clue about the quality of the soil. If their growth is stunted and their leaves discoloured then the soil is lacking minerals. Specific minerals can be applied for specific symptoms but here we are aiming for general soil fertility and we are giving the soil as wide a range of minerals as we can.

When money is a limiting factor, bulk buying among neighbours can be useful as the bigger quantity you buy, the cheaper it is, and most garden materials will store safely for years. Also, get your garden centre to stock the products you want by creating a demand for them.

1. The compact *Rotol* bin keeps compost to a manageable size.

2. Brassica stems should be smashed before composting.

3. To turn compost remove bin and fork over to introduce more air.

| Compost can be matured beneath sacking topped with polythene. | Neat compost heap boards are lifted as the heap is built. |

To start the organic garden going with mushroom compost is quite acceptable, but beware of bagged manure which comes from factory farming sources because it is mainly derived from stock fed or treated with hormones and other drugs that may end up as residues in the manure. Unfortunately, heat treatment does not destroy these undesirables, so be careful. There is no point in lavishing large quantities of humus on the soils if it also means introducing chemical drugs into the gardening cycle.

In this quick, short-term method of going organic, there still remains another important soil ingredient which has to be obtained. This is nitrogen, but we must be careful to get the right source. It might be tempting to use the chemical nitrogen fertilizers but these bring many undesirable consequences.

Nitrogen fertilizers result in nitrites in the soil which can enter the food chain through plants or leach into waterways and pollute our drinking water. With increasing concern about nitrites causing cancers we want to keep chemical nitrogen fertilizers out of the organic garden.

I much prefer an organic source of nitrogen such as a product called *Back-to-Nature* made by Pan Britannica Industries. The nitrogen content of this mixed soil-dressing comes from chicken manure guaranteed free from hormones and steroids. It also contains untreated Chilean potassium nitrate. Normally

I would not recommend this in a 100 per cent organic garden, but just for this quick-term policy it is ideal as it has not been processed in a chemical laboratory. It also contains a generous amount of essential minerals such as iodine, molybdenum, manganese, potassium and phosphate.

However, even this is not enough to cover the broad range of minerals needed for human health and which we hope to obtain from our diet. Unless these minerals are in the soil there is no way that they can reach us through the vegetables we eat. Many people have, in my opinion, no option other than to supplement their diet with minerals in tablet form, but the most lasting and beneficial form

Store autumn leaves in a wire cage lined with polythene.

Get rid of weeds — cover ground with calcified seaweed, followed by overlapping cardboard.

Top cardboard with black polythene, held in position with bricks.

of health comes from living on food which contains all the minerals we require.

That is another reason why I recommended using calcified seaweed.

A good dressing of this valuable powder will bring to the soil valuable quantities of calcium, magnesium, iron, iodine, manganese and small amounts of copper, zinc, cobalt, boron, chromium, nickel, sulphur and phosphorus. Combining both *Back-to-Nature* and calcified seaweed will make the average bag of chemical fertilizer look pathetic in comparison!

Making compost

GETTING off to a flying start with bought-in produce does take the pressure off the immediate need for compost-making, but there is no getting away from the fact that in the long-term large quantities of compost have got to form the backbone of any organic garden.

Compost is relatively simple to make. A few barrow-loads of rubbish dumped in a garden corner will eventually turn into compost, but results will quickly show that such heedless methods are not enough to grow crops of high quality. I soon learned that badly made compost reintroduces weeds faster than windblown seeds.

The old masters of compost-making always wrote about the technique of turning compost heaps so that the outside of the old heaps

Autumn mulch made from a good covering of sedge peat and pulverized bark.

Well-rotted leaves also make a good autumn mulch.

The early Brussels sprouts plot covered with rotted compost which is rotavated into the top few inches.

Brussels sprouts crop in production.

formed the inside of the new heap. But the days of leisure and pleasure in turning large compost heaps are over.

When I acquired my first *Rotol* bin, I discovered a far easier way of making good compost. There was no longer any need to make compost heaps 10 feet wide and 20 feet long (3m×6m). The compact *Rotol* bin allowed me to build smaller heaps quickly. The walls of the bin kept the heat in and there was no need to worry about the outside of the heap getting too cold to rot down. Due to the exterior protection, the combustion temperature inside could rise to 140-150°F (60-65°C); the temperature which destroys all weed seeds.

From research carried out at Birmingham University I discovered that a heap of rotting vegetation will exhaust all its air within seven to ten days. Thereafter the rotting process slows down quite dramatically. Putting this research to practical use was simple with the *Rotol* bin. Every seven to ten days I lifted off the cone-shaped bin and placed it about a foot away from the heap. Fluffing up the uncovered heap back into the bin, a forkful at a time was not too strenuous and the speed with which the heap heated up after the first turning confirmed the findings of Birmingham University. Fresh air was introduced and a second combustion took place. Within two weeks the shrinkage of the heap was phenomenal. And because the heap had been put through two heating-up processes, weed

The organic answer to weed and grass suppression beneath fruit trees results in friable compost which can be used later to mulch vegetables.

seeds were bound to perish.

I build the heaps up in layers, never more than nine inches deep. I use discarded fruit and vegetables from greengrocers, followed by grass cuttings which in turn can be followed by weeds and then garden vegetable waste. The important point to remember is to give each layer a dusting of either calcified seaweed or seaweed meal to make sure that all the compost contains a wide range of minerals. Spread between rows of plants or lightly forked into the top of the soil, I find the leaves of garden crops soon shine with good health.

This easy way of making compost means production can be stepped up. I found that two bins of fresh waste shrink so much after turning that they then fill only one bin. Although not absolutely necessary, the temptation is very strong to acquire a third bin which I did so that I could develop a system of filling two bins simultaneously. I used a *Compostabin* in addition to the *Rotol* bin. A week or so later the shrunken contents of both bins were turned into the third bin.

Once the system got under way it was an excellent compost production line. Whenever the third bin was needed, I emptied its contents into a neat heap and stored it until required for use. Any leaching during this storage period was prevented by a few sacks or old carpets thrown over as a covering topped with black polythene. With three bins on the go, it was amazing how much compost was manufactured in a relatively small space. The rotting process was very obvious when the compost left the third bin.

The efficiency of the system is due entirely to reactivating the compost with a new dose of fresh air every seven to ten days at the time of turning, and to the fact that the bin is filled fairly quickly in the first place. The habit of tipping odd bits of compost material into the bin is fraught with pitfalls, the worst one being that heaps built in this fashion seldom, if ever, heat up. I have always had the best results by saving all my waste materials in heaps

1. Successive layers of grass and paper act as a good fruit tree mulch.

2. Making wood ash in an incinerator is an excellent way of generating potash.

3. Burn only on windy days when smoke is dispersed and extinguish fires at night.

1. Inherited a weedy allotment?

2. Start by rotavating, then mulch with cardboard and polythene.

3. By spring plants can be put in through the mulch ready for a good harvest.

or in the case of vegetable waste, in polythene sacks, until there is enough to build the layers in the *Rotol* bin all in one go. This gives the forces of combustion a better chance to get going.

The bin method is ideal for the spring to autumn season when there is plenty of waste material about and the seasonal warmth helps maintain heaps at the correct temperatures.

Winter compost

IT is a pity that so many organic gardeners cease making compost through the winter due to lack of materials because an intensive organic garden can never keep up with the insatiable demand for humus.

I have tried using shop waste from greengrocers as the main compost ingredient during the winter months but this does pose problems because of its high water content. It also smells. But I didn't have to put up with it for long because I soon discovered that nature herself could make good compost from shop waste without much help.

This method has become a favourite of mine. After first spreading calcified seaweed over the ground, 2-16oz (50-450g) to the sq yd (m²), I worked methodically across the garden piling the shop waste, or even garden waste, six inches high. I covered this with cardboard or newspaper and then darkened the lot by covering everything with a sheet of strong black polythene. The sheet was weighted down by strong polythene bags partially filled with soil or sand. Using this method there was no smell or annoyance to neighbours.

All through the winter, underneath the sheet, the piled-up material rotted away to result in a friable humus in the spring. I found it was easy to part the humus to make a row and then sow or plant directly into the exposed soil beneath. I do not work this sort of compost into the soil for fear of upsetting the nitrogen balance. When left on top bacteria and worms continue to convert the underneath into plant food.

Part 3

Steps to successful seed sowing

SEED sowing is one of the most exciting and important jobs for the gardener. It is a job I never skimp, no matter when my seeds are sown. I look on February as the beginning of the season for seed sowing indoors. It is a time when light increases, and if frost penetration can be avoided, then most seeds will germinate readily.

Another reason why I delay sowing my seeds until February is the hope that outdoor temperatures will rise by the time seedlings are ready to be transplanted, so there is no danger of frost.

Nothing will grow in soil which is cold or frozen. That is why I find the *Ambig Seed-Raiser* so handy. The Ambig dish is only six inches (15cm) wide so several can sit on the window ledge of my south-facing front room. It is a room which is kept heated and therefore very suitable for raising seedlings. I save a considerable amount of money by not heating a 12 foot by 8 foot (3.6×2.4m) greenhouse for seed-raising, when I can raise them in hundreds on my window ledge instead.

However, more space is needed for transplanting, so the freshly pricked-out seedlings are then transferred to their greenhouse growing quarters. Cabbage, cauliflower, lettuce and onions have all thrived in the *Ambig* raisers. I cannot remember any of my seedlings ever suffering from mildew or other fungus problems that can affect freshly germinated seeds. This organic gardening method is far superior to the chemical alternative.

I am sure the capillary action of the *Ambig Seed-Raiser* contributes to this disease immunity. A capillary wick sucking up water from a reservoir is much better than watering from above. But I still feel that my organic growing mixture must take most of the credit for keeping growth so healthy and vigorous.

The formula for my seed and potting mix is always kept the same. I take two

1. Money can be saved by raising seedlings on a sunny window sill in the *Ambig Seed-Raiser* rather than heating a greenhouse for the job.

2. Watering is more efficient with a capillary wick. Here pots are three-quarters filled with loam and peat, top quarter filled with potting soil. The same pots (right) are soaking up water to ensure strong growth of onion seedlings.

3. A low-voltage propagating tray.

1. Propagating with low voltage trays while seedlings of squashes, marrows and cucumbers are ready for transplanting.

2. Pot-on seedlings in *A&D* polystyrene trays placed on *Corvex* boards to prevent roots from emerging and rooting into the soil.

3. Lettuce seeds are raised in the *Ambig Seed-Raiser* and potted on into *A&D* trays. Below (4.) the same seedlings show good strong growth.

parts of well-rotted compost, add one part of peat, one part of *Perlite* and mix well. I then add magnesium limestone to raise the pH to 6.8. I use a *Sudbury Soil-Test Kit* to check this. Calcified seaweed and seaweed-meal is already incorporated into the compost. These mineral-rich products were dusted onto the compost waste when the heaps were constructed. Seeds and seedlings grown with a wide range of essential minerals seem to resist disease. And the same observation has been noticed in people who live on food grown on mineral-rich soils.

I was introduced to an interesting new method of making potting compost by Mr John Purton. He discovered that the nitrogen contained in comfrey leaves could be trapped if the leaves were chopped and immediately covered with peat. When I tried his method I was quite impressed with the friable compost produced. The idea also included wrapping a black polythene sheet around the mixture to exclude light because this prevented the comfrey leaves from rooting in the peat.

Comfrey grows quickly after each cut. I often take five cuttings from each plant during the growing season, which is quite a lot of leaves. This growth capacity means that I can keep adding fresh leaves and peat on top of the last cuttings. I have made up my own formula, by dusting rock phosphate onto Mr Purton's mixture while the heap was being built. The number of oversize manure worms visible in the heap as the season progressed proved the value of this mixture.

When sowing seeds, however, it is important to choose a variety suitable for the period when one hopes to harvest the crop. Therefore all my early sowings are made with early varieties which should mature when prices are high. For example, Dobies Hispi Cabbage is sown during February so it will mature when prices are high. But choosing a main crop variety like Minicole can mean waiting for ages while it grows to make a very tight cannon ball heart. Minicole is a marvellous cabbage, but all the advantage

Make the most of greenhouse space by arranging plants at different stages, gradually filling up the entire area for maximum benefit.

Runner beans growing well in early June have benefited from early staking in pots. Note the mulch of newspapers to keep the moisture in.

of sowing seeds in a protective situation is lost.

Maximizing greenhouse space

THOUGH February sees the start of seed-sowing with the *Ambig Seed-Raiser,* when March arrives I transfer sowing to the floor of my cold greenhouse or under frames. I do not use compost-mix as the soil in my greenhouse is a friable mixture. Seeds sown in the friable humus and soil, which last season grew tomatoes, cucumbers and also received an autumn dressing of compost, will grow well.

Brussels sprouts, cabbage, cauliflower, calabrese and early leek seeds are sown in areas separate from any maturing crops. To maximize greenhouse space the plants should be at different stages. For example, while my seedlings are germinating on the greenhouse floor, my potted-on seedlings are resting on narrow platforms above them.

The trays I use for potting-on are called *A & D* polystyrene trays. So they can be picked up easily the inventor constructed a 40-section tray with a thicker wall down the centre.

I never sterilize any trays; a quick wash is all they receive from one year to the next. I believe that immunity to disease comes through attention to detail. For example, when transplanting seedlings I always handle each seedling by the seed leaf. I know from experience that handling the stem of young seedlings can bring on disease; it is also easy to fracture the stem by inadvertently squeezing it. Lettuce is very prone to this problem.

Another cause of disease is the bending of roots at transplanting operations. To avoid such an error I make sure the hole is deep enough so that roots stay straight. Potting-on seedlings is a job which shouldn't be rushed.

Occasionally I sow seeds directly into polystyrene trays, whenever space allows as this eliminates potting-on. But although I use pelleted seed, it may mean empty spaces, as it is not possible to get

100 per cent germination every time.

The *Corvex* boards that I place underneath each tray serve two purposes. It makes moving the trays easier but, more importantly, it also prevents roots emerging from the base and rooting into the soil. Trays of plants that have rooted into the soil are never successful. When the seedlings are moved the roots are left in the soil, slowing down the plant's growth as the roots have to regrow.

March to May the greenhouse is crowded with plants, but from April onwards I begin setting plants outdoors in sheltered spots, while still more plants are being raised in the greenhouse.

Frames also feature in my garden as this is a superb form of forcing. Again I prepare the soil in the autumn for cropping the following season. I never cover the soil with glass until a week or so before sowing or planting. The more moisture that can be trapped in the ground, the less one needs to water. My glass frames are constructed to slope down from nine inches on the north side to four and a half inches on the south side. This is a traditional method of trapping the light rays when the sun is low in the sky. Frames with high sides cannot possibly do this. I know that the height of mine is insufficient for high growing crops, but this has never been a problem. By the time the tops of crops like carrot touch the glass I remove the frames and cover with one of the new porous plastic nettings now available in garden centres. To gain height I erect a framework around the bed for the netting to rest on. While I prefer using modern telescopic aluminium tubes for this, in the past I have achieved the same result by stretching across wire nailed to the top of posts which have been knocked into the soil.

Peas, broad beans and runner beans can all be sown in pots in January, February and March for early crops. Here peas are shown in *A&D* trays (1.) while (2.), the same plants are at an early growth stage and finally in flower (3.).

Onion sets raised in a cold greenhouse are transplanted into the open (4.). The same crop maturing well (5.).

Handle seedlings by the leaf (right) to avoid damage. The stems of lettuce, cauliflower and cabbage seedlings should not be held when translanting.

Sowing outdoors

ONCE the season advances into May I sow directly into the ground. When I first started gardening my garden soil was in an impoverished state; seed-sowing into this poor soil always caused problems of bad germination, but then I introduced the idea of the V-trench. This involved digging a V-shaped trench three inches deep and filling the V space with prepared potting-mix. Once levelled and firmed seeds germinated well, because the roots were surrounded by a soil rich in nutrients.

One season I grew five crops of radishes in one V-trench proving that using the V-trench overcomes the problem of making sufficient compost to

Make a little compost go a long way with the V-trench method. The trench (above) is filled with compost, levelled and then firmed. Seeds like these radishes (right) germinate well surrounded by the rich nutritious compost. The radishes are pulled; it is possible to grow five crops in one trench.

garden organically. In addition to using only a small amount of compost, the V-trench can overcome drought conditions. Instead of watering large areas of soil to germinate a row of seeds, I do the opposite. I simply take out a V-trench and water this area thoroughly. I allow 24 hours for the wet to percolate into the soil before levelling and sowing the seed. This is a job which I always carry out in the cool of the evening to avoid any loss of moisture while I rake and prepare the seed bed.

Once the seeds have germinated, I mulch the space between the rows as an extra way of preserving moisture. This combination beats the drought and when water is in short supply it can safeguard the continuity of vegetable supplies.

Often birds are a threat to crops, but when this happens crops are easily protected by laying porous netting on the crop. No harm results and I remove the netting once the vegetables start growing on.

Part 4

Golden rules for growing under glass

HOW to keep up adequate supplies of organically grown foods in a British climate has puzzled many a good grower. Without introducing a few aids, it is impossible to fill the gap in vegetables when over-wintered outdoor supplies begin running short and the new crops are not yet ready. The easiest way, of course, is to have a greenhouse. These sturdy structures trap any stray ray of sunshine and they also protect the vegetables from cold winds, allowing the plants to grow.

I suspect one of the reasons why gardeners are reluctant to invest in a greenhouse is a fear of the unknown. It is an old wives' tale that once soil has been covered with glass then the grower must resort to chemicals to fight pests and disease.

In over 30 years I have never had any trouble in keeping my greenhouse crops free from disease. Despite using the same soil I have never sterilized it. The only standard I adopt is whether my soil remains healthy enough to grow produce that would keep the long-lived races of Ecuador, Caucasia and Hunzakuts in the healthy style to which they are accustomed.

The soil in my greenhouse has increased in fertility solely through added seaweed powders and organic kitchen waste. Anyone coming to my garden cannot fail to notice the line of dustbins close to the back door. They are there to provide organic household waste for the garden and they also have the added advantage of tight-fitting lids which are vermin-proof. Before a single seed is sown in my greenhouse these dustbins supply all the humus needed to provide the right growing conditions. I have yet to have a bad crop even though I am constantly cropping the same soil in my greenhouse, year after year.

Good soil is essential for successful greenhouse growing. These healthy crops in different stages of growth bear this out.

1. White Latham celery always follows spring cabbage in my greenhouse, while (2.), lettuce and curly cress precede tomatoes.

3. Myatts Offenheim Compacta is sown outdoors in mid-August, planted indoors in early November and is ready in March or early April.

Cropping plan for the greenhouse

THE most important crop in my greenhouse is early carrots. In most greenhouses it is usually possible to sow carrots from September onwards which produces early carrots towards the end of spring, but sowing seed in my greenhouse before the end of January interferes with my fertility programme. This is because I would rather use the November, December and January months to feed the soil, but once the soil has been prepared then I begin cropping.

In my 12×8 foot (3.6×2.4m) greenhouse I can expect to grow at least five different vegetable crops without them interfering with the additional tall summer crops of cucumbers and tomatoes. Positioning these crops correctly is time well spent. For example, carrots can grow alongside tomatoes and cucumbers. Therefore on the first convenient root-sowing date at the end of January or in early February I sow four rows of carrots along the length of the greenhouse. The first double row starts six inches (15cm) in from each greenhouse side and the next double row is nine inches in from that.

Four rows of early carrots will yield a fair crop if left to grow a reasonable size. I use quick growing varieties for these early sowings. Two of my favourites are Amsterdam Forcing and Early Nantes. Both varieties yield high quality carrots.

One of the problems with sowing seeds inside a greenhouse is that every seed seems to grow. Therefore ruthless thinning has to be carried out regularly. Early Nantes will produce more carrots when grown in cramped quarters than Amsterdam Forcing, so thinning out should take this into account. The former can be left half an inch apart while Amsterdam Forcing needs to be spaced one inch (2.5cm) apart. Watering regularly, particularly when the weather is hot, will increase their size and yield.

Between the carrots I sow my first rows of radish seeds. Both vegetables mature at different times. I choose the French Breakfast variety of radish as the leaves tend to grow upright and take up less space compared with the all-red varieties. Sowing the seed very shallow always brings me the best radishes. So, to get the right depth, I use a length of rope to make an impression in the soil by stamping along it. Once the seed is thinly sown in this indented impression. I cover it lightly with the adjoining soil. This is then firmed with a piece of flat wood to encourage rapid germination.

I am then left with an unplanted area of 12 feet × 5 feet 6 inches (3.6×1.6m). This never seems big enough for all the vegetables I want to grow, so I am forced to choose. My first choice is deciding how many crops I can grow before tomato and cucumber planting time. After a few years of trying different combinations I finally have a favourite cropping plan which includes lettuce, onion and beetroot. I put the beetroot at the far end of the greenhouse where they can be left until the middle of June before being cleared; for this purpose I like the quick growing variety, Bolthardy. When grown on a humus-rich soil, the quality is superb.

I allow myself the luxury of three rows, so nine inches (23cm) in from the far end I sow the first row across the greenhouse from carrot-row to carrot-row followed by two more rows each spaced nine inches (23cm) apart. Seedlings need to be thinned out to a distance of four inches (11cm) apart as soon as they are sturdy enough to handle. Beetroot doesn't grow well if it is sown early. Consequently, I mark out the beetroot rows with small sticks, and the seed is not sown until March.

The beetroot area reduces the central area to nine foot (2.7m), because I allow a further nine inches (23cm) of space before I fill the next five rows with onions. These onion rows are spaced six inches (15cm) apart. I don't leave this crop in the ground for long because if they are not

1. Keep out draughts by erecting a screen across doorways.

2. Seedlings are potted on at the rear.

3. Carrots, my most important greenhouse crop, grow underneath various vegetables raised in paper pots and resting on tubular supports.

1. Planting nasturtium and tagetes helps to keep white fly at bay.

2. Recycling domestic waste provides a vital source of humus.

3. The greenhouse floor is covered with domestic compost and the top two to three inches (5-8cm) is then forked in.

4. Dulce early potatoes are set out 12 inches by 12 inches (55×55cm), ready to be covered with garden compost and then topped with fruit tree mulch.

harvested when at the size of chives, they continue to bulb up and the flavour becomes a bit too strong to eat raw, though it's still marvellous for cooking. The variety which my family favours is Bedfordshire Champion. The tops of this popular onion variety are mild and tasty and much appreciated chopped with cottage cheese. Onions grow well when sown fairly early. Therefore in my unheated greenhouse I find that a February sowing is ideal.

Lettuce is another crop which I always grow in my greenhouse in early spring. By sowing the seeds the previous November and growing them in pots, this gives me well-grown plants for setting out in early February and cutting in early spring so I fill the remaining area of the greenhouse with these.

A planting distance of eight inches × eight inches (21×21cm) is adequate to produce a good greenhouse lettuce, particularly if the variety is Reskia. I discovered this variety a few years ago and I find that it produces not only a fine looking lettuce in the greenhouse, but it does well outdoors, too. It grows rapidly, taking only ten days from when the seed is sown to reach potting size. It is also the first lettuce to heart outdoors from the sowings raised on my front room window-ledge.

WIth vegetables growing along the greenhouse sides and across the greenhouse, access could become difficult. But the problem is solved quite simply by placing stepping stones along the centre of the greenhouse. To accommodate my size 9½ shoes I place three bricks together every 36 inches (90cm) — a convenient distance for my stride. I do this after the onion seeds are sown and the lettuce safely planted. I lose a small amount of onion seed when I do this, but this is of small consequence compared to the advantages of the stepping stones.

Make space for tomatoes and cucumbers

BEFORE I begin harvesting the onions, carrots, beetroot, lettuce, etc, I have found that it is best to insert a few tiny sticks where the two final crops, tomatoes and cucumbers, are to be planted, to show me which crops need to be harvested first to make space for the tomato and cucumber plants. It doesn't matter if the tomatoes and cucumbers are planted next to onions, carrots, beetroot and lettuce which are still growing, by the time the tomatoes and cucumbers start growing most of the early crops, except for carrots, will have been harvested.

Marking the planting spots for the cucumber plants is very easy. Along a single line two feet (0.6m) in from the long edge of the greenhouse I plant cucumbers two feet six inches (0.75m) apart. But along the other long side of the greenhouse, tomatoes need to be planted in a double row. I set the back row 18 inches (46cm) away from the edge of the greenhouse, planting tomatoes 18 inches (46cm) apart and then plant the front row, leaving a distance of 15 inches (38cm) between the rows. The tomatoes in the front row are staggered to allow access to the back row.

Planting-up time is something that I choose carefully because these crops need a minimum night temperature of 50°F (10°C) and a day temperature of 60°F (16°C) and I will even pot them on into larger pots to keep them in a warm position, rather than put them into a greenhouse while the temperatures are too low.

The plants soon establish themselves as my greenhouse soil is full of humus. The preceding November I adopted the Dutch method of spreading half-rotted domestic waste from my dustbins on top of the greenhouse soil and forking it in a month later. Twice I repeat this, adding fresh applications of waste to the soil. By the time I sowed my onion, carrot and radish seeds in February and March, all

1. Cucumbers climb well in the greenhouse while humus covers the growing stems.

2. A side view of tomatoes with tagetes just showing above the greenhouse base.

the water has disappeared into the soil.

After planting-up tomatoes, cautious watering is imperative to avoid the plants growing so fast they become straggly and look like something out of Jack-and-the-Beanstalk, which means the trusses are too far apart. After the initial planting I only water around the base of plants and wait for two trusses to form before increasing the quantity of water and watering the whole area.

Cucumbers, however, want plenty of water straight away. But more importantly, I encourage fresh roots to grow from the stem by continually piling half-rotted compost against the stems as the season progresses; and give them regular seaweed foliar feeds and a small amount of *Back-to-Nature* organic fertilizer.

Foliar feeding can work wonders with plants and the ingredient that I use most is liquid seaweed. Both *Maxicrop* and *Marinure* are excellent for this job and diluted 1:300 are really economical. Plants given regular doses of liquid seaweed become immune to the black fly and the green fly attacks. During the previous January powdered seaweed should be forked into the top few inches of the soil.

Another pest which I no longer have any problems with is white fly. This pest is repelled by the smell of tagetes and nasturtium, so, because I sow nasturtium seeds in the four corners of my greenhouse in April and I plant

A peep at the goodies in the greenhouse with tomatoes planted between onions, carrots and beetroot.

tagetes along the length of the carrot rows every time the pulled carrots leave a space, the plants in my greenhouse are never affected by white fly.

Finally I make sure that the greenhouse is well ventilated, one burst of the sun can send the temperature soaring. Most greenhouses are inadequately ventilated and mine is no exception. I leave my greenhouse door open during all hot weather but leave a polythene screen across the lower third of the doorway to prevent draught.

Although I have described my favourite cropping plan, there are many other variations. Choosing your own is fun.

Part 5

Outdoor vegetable growing

UNDERSTANDING the connection between fibre and good health has been a big step forward in the last few years. Most people automatically think of bran as the best source of fibre, yet it is also found in fruit and vegetables. Green cabbage, unpeeled potatoes, swedes, turnips and parsnips as well as carrots, are good sources of fibre.

But there is a drawback; while enjoying the benefit of fibre from carrots, who wants to ingest the pesticides that creep into our flesh, fat and organs from factory-farmed carrots? The idea of over-sprayed vegetables forming part of our diet is certainly not a happy one. My answer is UDI — unilateral declaration of independence; self-sufficiency or nothing.

But planning vegetable supplies for 52 weeks is not easy. The key is to not lose enthusiasm once the season starts. It is all too easy to sow in good time, plant early maturing produce and then stop.

This is where a diary is essential. While the crop grows include the the date of sowing, distance thinned, how many rows, whether the crop was hit by drought or a cold spell, killed by frost, affected by slugs or pigeons, date of maturing, and information on yield and quality. These notes can be referred to and the same mistakes avoided next year.

The target is always the same: a steady supply of vegetables for cooking and for salads. There is a priority list of vegetables which should never be overlooked. Salads, for example, must be varied so I grow as much as possible of the following: tomatoes, cucumbers, lettuce, onions, radishes, celery, beetroot and carrots, all good sources of fibre, vitamins and minerals. Vegetables are needed in greater quantities. Cooking reduces their bulk so more fibre is eaten. It is vital to have plenty of the following vegetables growing or stored throughout the year: potatoes, spring greens, early summer cabbage, Brussels sprouts, swedes, peas, onions, parsnips and carrots.

1. Intercropping makes the maximum use of the garden: onions (left row) and lettuce (right row) grow between the sprout plants, while between the rows of sprouts a row of calabrese broccoli is planted.

2. After clearing the soil, the area is planted with sprouts, lettuce and calabrese. The stakes are to tie the sprouts.

Many other vegetables are useful but they take up a lot of space, sweetcorn, runner beans, cauliflower and calabrese, for example. Unless enough time and space are available, then resist these.

In a cold wet spring, germination can be erratic. This has taught me to proceed with caution when favourable sowing periods appear very early in the season. Long hard spells could easily follow, ruining germination. But a few rows sown outdoors early are an interesting gamble.

Intercropping Brussels sprouts

BRUSSELS sprouts are a useful crop. The picking season starts in August and continues until late spring. This remarkably long period of cropping is achieved by growing three varieties tailored to mature at different times. I grow the early variety of Peer Gynt, the mid-season variety of Citadel and late variety of Archilles. Of course the times of maturity will vary according to the season, but all have one thing in common: new fresh shoots wil grow from the stem, particularly from any blemished sprouts remaining on the stem unpicked. These tasty shoots add many weeks to the length of the sprout season, and my family relishes anything green growing from a Brussels sprout plant: sprouts, tops, shoots — the lot!

This crop needs careful attention. Once

1. In autumn the area is dusted with calcified seaweed (left). By springtime weeds start to appear (right).

2. The trenches are filled with compost and the plants earthed up as protection against cabbage root fly.

3. Sprout stems covered with black polythene yield marvellous potting compost (left). Without net protection plants are pecked by pigeons.

4. After the interplanted vegetables have been cleared the sprouts grow to fill the area.

potatoes have finished in the autumn, heavy dressings of compost from vegetable waste should be applied unstintingly. Minerals are supplied by dressings of calcified seaweed and seaweed meal, both used at the rate of 4oz per square yard (100g/m²), or more according to needs. Then a light forking over completes the spring-time cultivation. The aim is to achieve firm, solid planting conditions to avoid the plants rocking about in wintry weather because the ground is too loose.

Sowing the seed promptly is essential, too. Be it early, mid-season or late varieties, all are sown at exactly the same time. I sow Brussels sprouts in late February in trays which remain on my window-ledge until they are pricking-out size. Then the seedlings are put outdoors in *A & D* polystyrene trays, under glass protection until a good planting-out time arrives, from the middle of April onwards. This should be done as soon as the soil becomes friable. Planting up when the soil is soggy and wet is inadvisable.

I used to plant Brussels sprouts in rows spaced 24 inches (60cm) apart with the plants spaced 24 inches (60cm) along the rows, then it occurred to me that much of this space could be used for growing early crops before the space was needed by the tall-growing sprouts. Over successive years, I have squeezed in many other crops, including peas, spring onions and even summer cabbage. But the list can be extended, if time and labour are available to include lettuce, carrots, radishes and calabrese. But remember it is harder work to keep the area properly cultivated when more crops are squeezed in.

In recent years I have established a planting distance of 33 inches (84cm) between rows and 24 inches (60cm) between each sprout plant. By the time I have finished marking out where everything will grow, the area looks a forest of tiny sticks. The long rows are spaced 16½ inches (42cm) apart and along alternate rows, I place sticks 24 inches (60cm) apart. Once this has been

1. Dustings of black pepper deter mice (left) while *Papronet* covering (right) protects plants from bad weather and stimulates growth.

2. Peas (left), cabbage (middle) and sprouts (right) fill the growing space.

3. This Hispi variety of cabbage (left) is ready for cutting, leaving space for growing sprouts (right).

done everything fits into place. The first crop to occupy my sprout plot are peas. I choose a low-growing variety which requires the minimum of staking, Feltham First. These are sown from the middle of February, quite closely, less than an inch apart, along some empty stickless, alternate rows. I aim to have peas growing on each side of sprouts. Sprouts benefit from peas growing nearby, because peas gather nitrogen from the air and deposit it in their root nodules and then in the soil.

The rows not sown with peas can support early summer cabbage or spring onions. Onions need to be sown very early in March because they take time to germinate. I like Bedfordshire Champion as they have always proved reliable and tasty as spring onions and if left unpicked will produce acceptable onions.

The only variety of summer cabbage that I use for intercropping with sprouts is Hispi. They grow upright, do not sprawl and can be

These beautiful early summer cauliflowers grew among the sprouts.

quickly cut and cleared before the growing sprouts demand more space. Early February is the best time to sow Hispi. A temperature of 60°F (16°C) in the first few days after sowing the seed will guarantee quick germination and subsequent growth. Potting-on takes place about ten days after sowing the seed. I choose my planting-out time with care, to avoid a severe check. Even so, covering the plants with a porous plastic sheeting like *Papronet* will protect them from bad weather. The sheet needs to be removed once the plants start growing.

I have mentioned three crops that can be grown between sprout rows, but there is also 24 inches (60cm) between each plant that can be similarly cropped. Radishes sown early in March will germinate and be harvested within six to eight weeks. Early French Breakfast Forcing is ideal for this. Lettuce is another crop which can grow between each sprout plant without interfering with the growth. I use upright varieties for this purpose. Winter Density is one favourite, which I sow in trays on my window-ledge in January. However, Reskia (a round variety) sown early in February and potted-on later in the month, can also be transplanted between the marked sticks to mature without disturbance.

Many other vegetables lend themselves to this intercropping system but remember that all intercrops must be sown early so they have finished before the sprouts need the space. Such intensive cropping makes big demands on the soil so the ground will need heavy feeding.

This Citadel variety of Brussels sprouts shows remarkable growth without the use of chemicals.

My grandson, Philip, is holding a Myatts Offenheim Compacta which was grown in a greenhouse, while growing in the background is the same variety which grew outdoors during a wet winter.

Spring greens which are protected by glass will be ready early and be of good quality.

Successful spring greens

WITHOUT the application of extra nitrogen once the winter has passed, I find spring cabbage a difficult crop to grow. Neglecting spring cabbage after a wet winter is to invite a crop that will taste like leather boots. The leaves can become tough unless the plants are encouraged to grow rapidly. Adding 2oz to the square yard (50g/m²) of the organic fertilizer *Back-To-Nature* is helpful, as is nettle juice. A rain-tub full of nettle leaves with a weight on top of the leaves will squeeze the juice out so it can be caught in a bucket and either watered or sprayed on the spring cabbage crop. The liquid needs to be diluted one to ten. To maximize the nettle juice I always add liquid seaweed one to 200.

In my area of Britain, Surrey, an excellent variety to grow is Myatts Offenham Compacta. The crop does well in most years and fills part of the gap between the old and new Brussels sprout crop. This means that I sow my seeds between August 7-14 to enable the plants to be transplanted and well established before winter sets in. It is no good applying nitrogen at this stage because it might make the plants too soft to withstand heavy winter frosts. Spring greens do well after early runner beans and so planting them out 12 inches × 12 inches (30×30cm) they fit neatly in with the mulched but vacated runner bean rows. Covering the growing crop with netting against wood pigeons is a must, as these marauders hack any unprotected crop to pieces if left undefended.

As soon as the weather improves I aim to get my spring greens growing quickly. Hoeing the soil to let in fresh air is a great help. Nothing grows if the soil is soggy. Many people allow spring greens to grow into very hearty cabbage, but the early summer cabbage variety, Hispi, grows so quickly that I have a very good succession of greens for eating. I start with the over-wintered Myatts Offenham Compacta as greens, followed by the young succulent Hispi when it has hearted up ready for cutting. I leave the remaining Myatts Offenham Compacta to continue hearting up. After eating Hispi cabbage my family starts again on the now mature, hearted Myatts Offenham Compacta cabbage.

When I sow the seed for Hispi cabbage in

Spring cabbage in February, surrounded by walls to deter rabbits and covered by netting to protect it from pigeons.

early February it goes into trays on my window-ledge where I can keep it at 60°F (16°C). I prick them out after ten days into *A & D* trays to leave them protected under glass outdoors. At transplanting time I bear in mind that fewer of the Hispi cabbage are needed than Myatts Offenham Compacta, but this will be a valuable entry for your gardening diary.

Part 6

The roots of good health

THERE is an alternative to poor health. Good health relies on an adequate supply of vitamins and minerals daily and, happily, root vegetables including beetroot, carrots, and swedes provide these in good measure. I always ensure that there are plenty of root vegetables in my garden to see me through the winter.

But there are two points to remember. Root vegetables will garner in our valuable minerals for us, but the minerals have to be available initially. In other words, if the soil lacks minerals then the root crop will also be deficient. The second point is preparation. Root vegetables grated or cut up and left uncovered before eating will rapidly lose their vitamin content. Nothing is grated or shredded in my house until the moment before eating. Many attractive meals can be conjured up with root vegetables by adding sprouts which I grow on my window-ledge, while grated apple and raisins are two other ingredients I enjoy.

Beetroot is a real stand-by. Grated or cooked, eaten hot or cold, grown correctly, this root is full of natural sugar.

Problems can arise in growing beetroot if the soil conditions are adverse. A cold wet spring can play havoc if the wrong varieties of beetroot are sown. Recently all my early sowings have been of the Bolthardy variety. This is an excellent beetroot for growing early in the season. Although the flesh is not as fine as Detroit, it is a fast grower and not so likely to go to seed. I sow this variety from the end of April up to the beginning of May either in cold frames or outdoors. Then it is time for the main crop varieties. I usually choose Detroit (round), but I also grow Cylindra (half tall) and Cheltenham Green Leaved (long tapering). All are excellent cooked, but I prefer Detroit for grating raw in salads.

Even when the weather warms up, beetroot seed can be very temperamental. When I grew commercially, I spaced the

Above: Shredded comfrey and nettle leaves ready for juicing. Dilute one part to ten to make an excellent foliar feed for all root vegetables.

Below: These Bolthardy beetroot (below) were left unthinned, resulting in small roots.

maincrop sowings over a four-week period. If one sowing didn't germinate then at least I had three more to rely on. I have carried this practice over into my garden. Small, frequent sowings are the golden rule, especially as this spreads out the job of thinning. But now I follow moon sowing dates. I choose the root phase according to this system, for sowing my beetroot seed. For example, *Working with the Stars 1984 Calendar* showed May 20, May 31, June 8, and June 17 as good root days. So these were the days I sowed my root vegetables, which included beetroot.

If the seed is sown too thickly, beetroot rows can resemble a forest of leaves, but in case germination is poor, I still resort to clump sowings. This means sowing two or three seeds every four inches, making thinning easy. Select the strongest seedling and hold it firmly between the fingers, and then pull away the surplus seedlings, not upwards but sideways. I choose a showery day for thinning as beetroot leaves tend to flop very quickly if disturbed.

A satisfactory distance between rows is 12 inches (30cm) but I prevent the beet

1. Beetroot leaves can be eaten if they are as healthy as this.

2. Growing beetroot on the same site for three consecutive years produced these discoloured leaves.

3. Sad-looking leaves of a crop grown on wet soil, deficient of nitrogen and minerals.

4. Seakale spinach is related to the beetroot, so do not follow one with the other.

5. Planting out sage next to rows of carrots is claimed to protect against the carrot-root fly but look at the disastrous results (6.).

7. Rows of carrots are guarded by onions and small pieces of rosemary are cut up and spread along the rows to ward off the carrot-root fly but again the results were disappointing.

1. Dusting carrots with powdered seaweed meal deters carrot-root fly.

2. Erecting a protective tent over carrots helps prevent the carrot-root fly from laying its eggs.

3. Mulching helps protect these carrots from infection while, in the background, unmulched carrots are surrounded by an anti-fly barrier.

from growing too large by restricting the distance along the rows to four to six inches (10-15cm).

I have found that beetroot grows well after a legume crop. The nitrogen left in the soil by the legume root nodules seems to be appreciated. Beetroot leaves clearly indicate the condition of the crop, when their healthy green quickly discolours. This could easily occur if the previous crop on that area was spinach, turnips, parsnips or carrots, since these all use up the same nutrients from the soil. It's nothing to worry about however, because I have seen this problem correct itself after a sprinkling of about 2oz to the square yard (50g/m²) of *Back-to-Nature* organic fertilizer plus a little calcified seaweed between the rows. This was prudently covered over with a mulch thick enough to keep the moisture in.

At the end of the growing season the reward for this attention to detail is delicious beetroot. But unless dug up and stored, beetroot can be decimated by frost. Although I've managed to avoid too much damage when caught out by a light frost, I see no point in keeping beetroot in the soil longer than necessary once autumn sets in. If short of time I simply twist the leaves away from the beet (I don't cut the leaves with scissors as this causes the beets to bleed). Then, I pile the beetroot up in a conical heap and place straw or old sacks over, which protects the pile from autumn frosts and keeps the beetroot moist. But towards the end of October, I take more positive steps about winter storage.

Beetroot clamped in the open preserves the best flavour but the box method has also served me well. It is simple and effective. I line a suitable box with black polythene and use capilliary or any other absorbent material as an inner lining before filling the box with beetroot. Storage has to be in a frost-free garage or room with easy access. Use this simple method to keep beetroot over the winter months or make a clamp.

Making a clamp outdoors involves building a conical heap of the chosen vegetable and covering it with a thick layer of straw, combing downwards. Soil is gradually applied to cover the straw. At least four to six inches (10-15cm) is left at the top to ventilate the clamp. This gives adequate protection against frosts. I leave a tunnel clear on the south side of the clamp, wide enough for my hand to enter and retrieve the beetroot. I cork this with a plug of removable straw. I choose dry days to retrieve what I need from the clamp. Pushing a hand along a narrow tunnel is quite messy in a downpour!

Coping with the carrot-root fly

CARROTS are a boon and a blessing to mankind if mankind will only let them. One of the benefits of eating a generous amount of carrots comes with improved night vision. This was brought home to me one very dark night when I was out walking with two companions. I noticed a telegraph pole looming ahead and shouted a warning — but neither could see anything. I think it would have been a different story if their daily diet included raw grated carrot in a salad and cooked carrot for dinner. But I don't just stop at that. For 45 years my Christmas pudding has had carrots as a main ingredient.

The greatest blessing of all must be the function of the pure, non-chemical carrot as an anti-cancer agent. Such is the demand for them that supplies are never adequate. It is imperative that carrots are grown without any chemical — so demand always exceeds supply.

Carrots were once grown by a large number of small growers as part of their crop rotation. This system meant that the likelihood of a pest build-up was small. Then DDT arrived. All fell before the onslaught of this powerful pesticide. Carrot-root fly disappeared. Growers became specialist in monoculture and the rotation method disappeared. Disaster struck. DDT no longer killed the carrot-root fly since a new, immune carrot-root fly had appeared. Scientists continued to dream up new, more

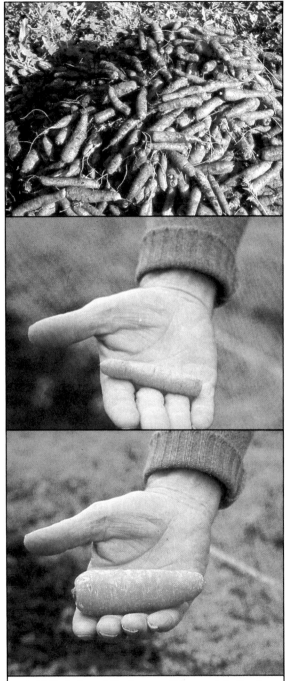

1. At first sign of fly damage it is much better to lift the crop and store in a clamp or to freeze.

2. Putting carrots to the test. Above, a chemically grown carrot is tested against this organically grown carrot (3.).

powerful pesticides. Carrots began to taste peculiar. Today the only way of ensuring carrots are safe to eat is for each of us to grow our own. The Organic Growers' Association tackle a gigantic task in distributing organically grown vegetables and they deserve our support. But the day of adequate supplies is a long way off.

It is our misfortune that in recent years growing carrots in the garden has been bedevilled with the arrival of a new super race of carrot-root fly. The result is a mass of dark holes that penetrate the carrots right through to the core so they become useless for eating. Carrot growing has now become a real fight.

All my early sowings of carrots go into the greenhouse or under cold frames; protected, there are no problems from carrot-root fly attack. This phenomenon has been researched by the Henry Doubleday Research Association. They confirmed that low polythene walls no higher than 2 feet 6 inches (76cm) act as a barrier against pest attacks. It was established that carrot-root flies are carried by the wind, unaided they do not travel well. Usually I keep all my outdoor carrot sowings covered with *Papronet* (a woven plastic sheet with micro-holes).

The *Papronet* was placed over the sowings and supported by portable sectional telescope tubes. This acts like a mosquito net and prevents the carrot-root fly from laying its eggs.

I have also tried another technique by dusting the crop with *Marinure* powder whenever the carrots were hoed or disturbed. I then extended this method by dusting weekly regardless. This may sound extravagant but it is worth every penny to obtain poison-free carrots. The machine I use blows out the seaweed powder very finely, thus keeping down the quantity used. However, careful observation will reveal the best methods of dealing with this vicious pest.

The main egg-laying periods stretch from late May to June, as well as July to August, according to official figures. Unfortunately my carrot-root flies are more vigorous, because I have suffered damage on carrots drilled in late September. The influence of the moon as well as the stars in growing root crops has been well documented. I try whenever possible to keep all my carrot sowings to the root days recommended in the *Working with the Stars 1984 Calendar.* Maria Thun who writes the calendar has been shown to be knowledgeable in her forecasts.

Carrots are thinly sown in rows 12 inches (30cm) apart, and such small seed can only be sown very shallow. Narrower spacing is feasible but needs more hand work to keep them clean. I aim to grow varieties like Nantes more thickly in the row than a wide-shoulder carrot like Chantenay. Carrots can grow huge if thinned to a distance of 6 inches × 12 inches (15×30cm). But my family prefer much smaller produce.

Swedes to be proud of

SWEDES thrive where there is moisture, good drainage and humus. Anybody looking at the lovely rich soils of Devon will understand why Devon swedes reign supreme in the market place. But to recreate Devonshire conditions in our back gardens is a tall order, particularly where soils are poor in humus and badly drained. But even so, it's much better to grow Devon swedes than to buy them!

I discovered that certain parts of my garden cannot grow swedes during a wet summer and autumn and rose to the challenge! I converted part of my garden to form beds one foot high so that drainage was no longer a problem and swedes as well as turnips could then look their Devon counterparts in the eye.

Devon growers who go for early maximum tonnage drill their swedes in early May. However, I very seldom drill before June and aim more towards the latter half of this month. Swedes as well as turnips need wider spacing as a way of allowing the air to circulate. My standard width is 18-inch (45cm) rows. Thinning the seedlings to nine inches (23cm) apart produces a root that is adequate for two to eat.

I use so much calcified seaweed that boron deficiency hardly comes my way. I dodge the flea beetle by sowing my swede or turnip seeds in well-watered soil. Under such conditions, and by sowing in the warmest months, germination is rapid. The flea beetle never bothers me as this pest thrives best on soils lacking in humus, which are allowed to become as dry as dust and then fertilized with chemical fertilizer.

Acme swedes and Golden Ball turnips are two good varieties. Both are tough enough to withstand frost so I seldom have to lift and store either although in severe weather I may store a small amount under a deep layer of straw.

Part 7

Potatoes worth growing

THERE was a time when most gardeners begrudged the garden space which potato-growing needed, because potatoes were so cheap and plentiful in the shops. But now the quality of the commercially grown crop has plummetted. No wonder it has become chips-with-everything, we have to fry them to give them any sort of taste.

An old farmer was the first to draw my attention to it. Where he grew up, the local people relied heavily on potatoes which they grew on seaweed gathered from the shores of Cumbria. A district nurse recalled much the same story about some impoverished families living off their own produce in the Channel Isles. Freshly gathered seaweed was all they used for growing their crops. These families were by far the healthiest folk of the district.

If we want our full quota of goodness from potatoes then we have to grow our own. Like all roots, potatoes store most of their minerals in or just under the skin. And just look at the list — vitamin C, phosphorus, potassium, calcium, iron, niacin, tin, vitamins B_1 and B_2, traces of copper and much else. Potatoes also supply vital fibre to keep the colon healthy.

As soon as the present crop is lifted my mind is already focusing on next year's crop. I select potatoes for next season's seed, store them in shallow wooden grape trays and keep them indoors away from frost, until a month or so before they are planted. Then I move the trays into the dark to encourage shoots to grow long and spidery. On the day before planting, they are brought back into the light to harden the shoots against breaking easily.

Several past experiments convinced me that potato seed planted with long spidery shoots will yield large size potatoes without decreasing the output. I prefer a smaller number of large potatoes to a larger number of small potatoes. I only save enough seed to plant half my proposed area and I buy the

1. Freshly cut comfrey leaves were placed in alternate trenches and gave cleaner potatoes and a greater yield.

2. The two rows on the right, grown with home seed for nine years, compare poorly to those on the left planted with home grown seed for the first time.

3. These plants have withstood the onslaught of six weeks of drought.

1. These no-dig-potatoes were grown under a mulch outdoors.

2. Long spidery shoots give more and bigger potatoes.

3. Plenty of compost was applied to this crop in my greenhouse.

4. Look at the deep green foliage of this potato crop of mine, growing on powdered seaweed.

remainder from reputable suppliers of Scotch/Irish virus-free seed, and I only take my own seed from this imported, virus-free seed.

Planting potato seed is one of the easiest jobs. Straight ridged-up rows, 24 inches (60cm) apart and seed placed 12 inches to 15 inches (30-46cm) apart along these rows, is the basis of my planting system. If given enough compost either shredded or sieved through a half-inch sieve, the seed need not necessarily be buried with soil. The trick is to keep on adding compost as the foliage grows. I have used this method on an indoor crop of early potatoes. How I loved retrieving handfuls of early potatoes from the soft compost mulch! No laborious digging was needed here.

Most of my potatoes are grown in the traditional way with one or two special differences. When the V-trenches have been drawn out 6-9 inches (15-23cm) deep, I fill up half the depth with mixed compost including grass cuttings, and into this mixture I place the seed potatoes. Then a further covering of a similar mixture completes the job. Over this sandwich I draw up the soil to form high ridges exacxtly over the seed.

The second trick is in the timing of the addition of minerals. I wait until the crop starts growing before I make the important applications of calcified seaweed, seaweed meal and *Back-to-Nature* organic fertilizer. I spread all these rich minerals in between the rows. I hoe the rows several times to ensure thorough mixing with the soil before I have finally finished drawing the ridges up higher and higher around the potato tops. I stop when the tops close over the rows.

Before lifting in the autumn the skins should be tested. Select a single potato from under the plant. If the skin doesn't come off when the thumb is rubbed hard along it, that means the skin is set hard and will keep during winter storage. If the skin comes away as in a new potato, this is too soon to lift the crop. When harvesting, let the potatoes dry out in the autumn sun for an hour, but too long in the sun turns them green. Then sort them into four piles: one with good undamaged potatoes for storage, another with slightly faulty produce to be used up first, the third comprises seed to be saved in trays. The remaining marble-sized potatoes in the fourth pile are destined for the compost heap!

There is a great satisfaction to be had in stacking away in a frost-free place your horde of nutritious potatoes, especially when you grow a variety to suit your own purpose. For me, a baked potato conjures up a most companionable picture for a winter's day, and therefore the bulk of my crop is Desiree, a tasty, floury potato. But for the occasions when I want to boil my potatoes, I grow Pentland Javelin, a more waxy potato which does not break up when boiled. But in ground where potatoes come out slug-ridden and covered in scab, then the best variety is Croft.

Italian lettuce are becoming more popular. Many can be overwintered to yield tasty leaves in the spring.

Easy ways with lettuce

THE first crop of lettuce I ever grew, tasted like soft cardboard. This wasn't surprising considering the poorness of the soil. I have come a long way since then, and have learned that a shallow V-trench, filled with precious compost, is quite sufficient to start the organic cycle. This, with minerals and a mulch around the growing plant, will produce wonderful growth in most soils. I can reassure beginners that the basic desire to grow organically is not difficult to fulfil when these simple methods are followed.

Over the years I have learned to be cautious with seed sowing plans in the early part of the year, because successive sowings were ready at the same time. This happened in spring 1984 when cold nights retarded all growth regardless of when planting took place. Anyone reading Covent Garden Market reports at that time would have realized that most commercial growers suffered from an over-production of lettuce, and this happened to home gardeners too. The secret of maintaining a steady supply of lettuce for the home is to sow little and often, with some protection as a safeguard. Surrounding the crop with a wall of *Papronet* or better still, with wire mesh reinforced polythene, 18 inches (45cm) high, makes quite a difference.

As with roots, I follow the recommended dates in the planting calendar. I plan to sow at least three times a month to fit in with leaf days. Using this method there are very few weeks in the lettuce-growing season when my garden hasn't a row of lettuce ready for cutting.

There are still some puzzling problems to overcome. Some varieties refuse to wake up when sown, and three months later, in among a cabbage crop, a perfect row of lettuce suddenly germinates. I tackle this peculiarity of lettuce by mixing the seed in with a little damp sand and storing it in a refrigerator for three or four days. The lettuce, of course, doesn't know it has been tricked into thinking winter

1. Salad Bowl lettuce yield masses of nutritious leaves that keep on coming.

2. Cobham Green lettuce are reliable and slow to bolt.

3. Look at the density of these Tom Thumb lettuce.

1. This row of Little Gem lettuce were growing in November and resisted autumn frosts.

2. Summer lettuce seedlings are best looked after by the back door.

3. Horace the toad and his relatives help to keep down the slug population.

1. Endive can outlast most lettuce for November cutting.

2. Corn salad leaves can be grown in most gardens. Sow in August or September for spring use.

I have always tried to transplant seedlings towards the cool of the evening, into rows that have been thoroughly watered the previous day. But if the soil still looks wet and puddly, then I wait another 24 hours. After planting the seedlings they are then immediately mulched so as to conserve all moisture. This method rarely fails.

Recently, a type of polythene has been available in garden centres, to allow lettuce plants to be planted into the soil through specially cut holes. This is ideal for people who are troubled with weeds. The polythene does save a tremendous amount of hand-weeding.

I seem to be constantly reading how slugs have become a menace in many gardens, but I feel sure that a lot of this can be avoided. At one time I could count as many as twenty slugs when cutting my lettuce, but in the last year or two, the appearance of even one is sufficient to arouse comment. I feel sure that my slug population is kept well under control by the many predators attracted into my garden now that my soil has been richly endowed with seaweed powders. Perhaps it is the sodium content of seaweed that is deterring the slugs. But then my frogs and toads must also receive credit for keeping the garden clean judging by the number of times I can spot them while I'm walking through the special areas which I allow to grow wild. Frogs and toads love wet clingy overgrown grass areas.

In my trial rows I have always been impressed by the little lettuce with a solid heart, Tom Thumb. This variety, planted 6 inches (15cm) each way, will produce more to the square foot than a larger conventional lettuce, needing at least 9 inches (23cm) square spacing. Nevertheless for the larger, crisp Cos lettuce, seed firms are still offering old favourites like Little Gem, Lobjoits Green Cos and Winter Density, all for sowing between spring-time and June, though later sowings of Winter Density can be over-wintered. But for occasions when only round cabbage lettuce is demanded, I sow the dark green Buttercrunch before June and dark green Avon-defiance after June.

Most of the time, lettuce benefit from applying liberal quantities of water in between

has passed. But this gives them the go-ahead to germinate, securing perfect germination almost every week.

I start the seeds off in the *Ambig Seed-Raiser,* producing enough seedlings to guarantee successive supplies. Also by potting on in *A & D* polystyrene trays, seedlings can be nurtured and looked after by the back door, especially when growing conditions can be dry and unsuitable outside.

two crucial stages. These are from when the plant starts growing until just before hearts start forming. Water applied before the plant starts growing away or after hearts start forming is liable to lead to a lot of rotting. Natural rain never seems to cause this problem. But cultural details of this crop are worth attention because life without lettuce for salads and sandwiches can seem empty.

Perfect parsnips

THE humble parsnip was at one time considered to be an essential part of the working-man's diet. Parsnip and cheese together supply much in the way of vitamins, minerals and protein which is what, after all, we want from food.

I always resist sowing my parsnip seed too early, simply because I hate having to handle large parsnips. Looking back in the gardening books, most contributors years ago advised that parsnip seeds should be sown during the early part of spring, say February/March. I save my parsnip sowings until the end of June. The rows are spaced 12 inches (15cm) apart, but I don't thin my plants out further than 4 inches (10cm). The resulting parsnip is just the size I want, but if you prefer a larger parsnip, sow earlier and allow more space between plants.

Avonresista parsnips have suited me very well, but I have been tempted once or twice to grow the Offenheim hollow-crowned parsnip as well as Cobham Improved. Both are remarkably sweet and grate easily for the

Good-sized parsnips from a late sowing of Cobham Improved.

winter salad, blending well with grated cheese.

I have never found the need to store or clamp parsnips as they keep remarkably well in the ground right through the cold winter months.

A trick I have used to prevent the parsnips from being ice-locked in the ground in very severe winters is to spread straw very thickly over the parsnip area. This prevents the ground from freezing.

Part 8

Organic methods of production suit tomatoes perfectly. This fine crop of Marshall's Red Alert was grown on polythene which covered a nourishing mixture of compost, seaweed meal, calcified seaweed and newspaper.

Top treatment for tomatoes

IT IS hard to think of a more popular food than the versatile tomato, yet its good texture and flavour soon deteriorate under adverse growing methods. Chemical methods, for example, are not to its liking.

I will never forget one particular customer from my business years when I used to invite buyers to pick their own vegetables from my field. He regularly picked runner beans and sometimes cut a marrow but he never went near the tomato house — he hated tomatoes. Then one day, while waiting in the queue to weigh his vegetables, he idly popped into his mouth one of the small slices of tomato put there for customers to sample.

He couldn't stop after that! He was hooked on organically grown tomatoes, and that is the fate of all organic gardeners once the tomatoes start ripening.

It is a skilled operation to get tomatoes to ripen early. Light and heat play a large part in encouraging sturdy growth, and this applies particularly to outdoor tomato growing because the season is so short. For example,

June-planted tomatoes should produce at least four trusses to make the project worthwhile. On the other hand, when tomato seed is planted too early the end product could well be a three-foot (92cm) tall plant, with not a truss in sight except near the top, for want of light.

Therefore, I sow my tomato seeds in March: daylight is beginning to increase and frosts are beginning to wane. At this time of year temperatures of 60°F (16°C) in the daytime and 50°F (10°C) at night will not be difficult to maintain with the help of a bit of cover.

There are now so many useful propagatory aids on the market that it is really a question of what one can afford. At the top end of the propagating frame market, heat, light and even watering devices are all cleverly integrated, complete with automation controls, but I have grown outdoor tomato plants from seeds germinated in the airing cupboard. These were subsequently sheltered on the south-facing window ledge and did well when planted outdoors. It's all a question of time versus money.

Germination of March-sown tomato seed is fairly rapid. I have seen seedlings appear in five days, but that was due to a night temperature of 70°F (21°C). With lower temperatures I expect to transplant into pots after 17 to 21 days. Spacing the plants to allow plenty of light to penetrate will guarantee a sturdy plant, and will allow fruit trusses to form low on the stem.

Compost for seed growing is easily manufactured using well-made garden compost which had plenty of seaweed minerals added during the compost-making process. In recent years I have discovered the value of comfrey leaves. Chopped up, mixed with peat and covered with black polythene this mixture soon rots into valuable potting material. A dash of magnesium limestone and a touch of *Back-to-Nature* fertilizer will grow plants free from disease, while drainage can be helped by also mixing in a small amount of *perlite*. I use one part of *perlite* to four parts compost.

The easiest part of tomato growing comes once they have been set outdoors. I allow 24 inches (60cm) between plants and once growth begins I provide a stout bamboo cane to each plant. Side-shooting is not a difficult job: once a week I remove the shoots growing at the spot where the leaf of the plant joins the main stem. Bending the shoot backwards is one method of removal, while a sharp knife also makes a neat removal job.

Splitting fruit, blotchy ripening, stem rot or blight can soon spoil a season's labour. At one time I kept the soil surrounding outdoor tomato plants free from weeds, but this caused problems. Experience and observation has shown me that mulch is the secret of immunity to plant disease.

I cover the soil around the plant fairly early in the season, and once again comfrey leaves do a wonderful job. I add to this mulch as the season advances, and it is one of nature's best anti-pest and anti-fungus protection. It is made up of grass cuttings with a wide range of weeds, all containing extra minerals to add to those I already applied to the ground.

1. These Yellow Perfection tomatoes look good but their flavour was disappointing.

2. A case of Jack and the Beanstalk! These sweet and good quality tomatoes are Unwins F¹ Hybrid.

3. I grew this crop in 1975 before I started mulching.

4. A look under the polythene mulch at the richness that now replaces the grass once growing on this area.

The advent of the new strain of bush tomatoes makes side-shooting and even mulching unnecessary. Last season I grew Marshall's Red Alert. I spread half-rotted domestic waste on an area of grass and then added four ounces (100g) each of calcified seaweed and seaweed meal to the square yard (m²), then covered this with newspaper and finally black polythene. This operation was carried out in mid-April, and about five to six weeks later I cut slits in the polythene, 18 inches (45cm) apart and set out the Red Alert tomato plants through the slits.

I picked the first fruit at the end of July and the flavour and taste would have been instantly recognized by anyone who could still remember what tomatoes once tasted like.

1. Big Boy tomatoes grown outside compare poorly to these (2.) grown in my greenhouse.

The surprising part about growing these tomatoes is that no water was applied to the crop at any time, even though record droughts were being suffered all over the country. The crop was grown on grassland which was covered merely seven weeks before the plants were set out.

Tomato growing is exciting but true success comes only with organic methods. Growing this crop organically and in the sunniest position available assures its full quota of vitamin C and bioflavonoids as well as vital minerals. These valuable nutrients can be easily lost when tomatoes are grown with chemicals.

Celery that's convenient

CELERY is not really at home in my dry, dusty Surrey soil, for it really loves the deep, moist soil of the Lincolnshire fenlands. But if I want to observe the age-old health advice of always including a leaf, a stalk and a root in my daily diet, then I feel that no amount of trouble is too much to coax a crop of celery out of my indifferent soil. This supplies me not only with the stalk but also green leaves for a tasty soup.

I first began growing celery in trenches. To blanch and tenderize the stems, the earth was drawn around them as they grew, so light didn't reach the stems until they were harvested. The introduction of self-blanching varieties was really labour-saving, because planting them close together meant that the stems were again blocked from the light.

In recent years, however, I have given priority to the American Green varieties, because of their resistance to autumn frosts, and I also find that the uncut American Green will throw fresh green shoots once spring gets under way, provided the area is covered with a protective layer of straw.

In early March I sow the seed of American Green varieties using the *Ambig Seed-Raiser.* I never cover celery seed once they have been sown, I rely on the capilliary stick of the *Ambig* to suck up water and keep the surface moist. It is useful at this stage to enclose the *Ambig* in a polythene tent, which conserves moisture and provides extra warmth. All this is carried out on the window ledge of a south-facing room.

Within six weeks I start potting-on and I use the *A & D* polystyrene trays until planting-out time. Happily, celery plants can be held in trays with impenetrable boards underneath until needed and it is very handy to be able to use celery to fill spaces as they appear. Two ounces (50g) of *Back-to-Nature* per square yard (m²), plus a mulch of compost is all the celery ground receives, and I plant out the American Green plants at a distance of 15 inches by 12 inches (38×30cm). This ground will produce really large celery, provided a steady nitrogen feed is given during growth.

The juice squeezed from nettles and grass cuttings yields a liquid rich in nitrogen. This

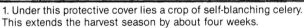

1. Under this protective cover lies a crop of self-blanching celery. This extends the harvest season by about four weeks.

2. Just look at the perfect leaves on this crop of American Green celery.

3. Growing celery in trenches is an excellent way of cutting Christmas celery, but it is a labour intensive method.

4. Celery is planted here in trenches prior to earthing up.

5. This American Green celery has been planted 12 inches (30cm) each way.

is obtained by placing chopped nettles and grass cuttings into a barrel with an open bung-hole. After leaving a heavy weight pressed on the nettles and grass for a couple of weeks, the liquid begins to ooze out of the bung-hole and into the waiting bucket underneath.

This concentrated liquid feed is diluted one:ten, and I also add liquid seaweed diluted at one:200. This is a sure way of keeping celery in good health and free from disease! The ground should be well-watered as celery does not tolerate dryness.

The curative properties of celery, especially in rheumatic ailments, means that celery has priority in my garden.

Cultivate cucumbers

CUCUMBERS enjoy being pampered. They positively thrive when grown in neat heaps of compost made from garden waste. If this compost is enriched with seaweed minerals plus a small amount of half-rotted manure then the result is a bumper crop.

My golden rule is to make the compost open so as to keep the plant free from surplus water. I prefer to sow cucumber seed in single pots. I firm the potting compost, then push the pointed end of the seed into the potting mixture. It doesn't matter if the blunt end is left protruding as long as the pots are kept moist and not allowed to dry out. I keep them sheltered until night temperatures rise, when I set them outdoors on the compost mounds. They will need a space of three feet (91cm) per plant.

Another good method for sowing a later crop direct in the ground is to lay the cucumber seed on damp blotting or kitchen paper and chit them in a warm cupboard. This gets over the problem of germination which is the most difficult part of cucumber growing. Once germinated I put three seeds, point downwards into each compost mound, and cover them with jam jars or a clear plastic tent. Then I simply choose the most sturdy seedling out of the three for growing on. It is important to avoid over-crowding, so thin them down to one plant per station as soon as possible. This is one way of guaranteeing a successful crop.

However, left to their own devices cucumber plants will produce a lot of uneven growth, and it can come as a shock to find they have run amok in next to no time. The art lies in pinching out the growing point as soon as the first leader produces six leaves and being ready for when the next leaders, which will grow from the joint between a leaf and the main leader, have also produced six leaves each. After pinching out their growing tips, I spread out these new leaders so the plant will yield cucumbers growing evenly from all sides. Burpee Hybrid is particularly good grown this way.

I have grown cucumbers to a size of six inches (15cm) long while other varieties can't seem to stop growing even after reaching three feet in length. The length is governed by its genes. Year by year plant breeders seem to increase their ability to dictate the cucumber's eventual growth and size as well as its quality.

In days gone by, all cucumbers which were pollinated grew with a coarse bulbous end, but now plant breeders have given us outdoor varieties which, though they need pollinating, grow well-shaped fruit without the bulbous end and also the outdoor cucumber's bitter taste. I grow my cucumbers outdoors, so pollination is not a problem, all the cucumbers are visited by bees and insects.

I never lose my fascination for the Kyoto, a Japanese cucumber. The length to which they can grow is phenomenal, yet each is pencil slim with a pleasant crunchy flavour. Unlike the other cucumbers, however, I found it best to tie the growth to stakes, so that the Kyoto cucumbers grow as straight as bamboo canes.

When growing cucumbers, feeding is terribly important. I like to increase the height of the growing mound by adding fresh compost as the season progresses. Additional layers of fresh compost will encourage new roots and this in turn means more cucumbers. A little *Back-to-Nature* in the fresh compost will ensure sufficient plant foods to keep everybody happy, including the plant.

More than once I have been grateful for the refreshing value of grated cucumber in soothing tired eyes. I enclose the grated

Beth Alpha Miracross is an outdoor cucumber with the flavour of an indoor cucumber. A separate male pollinator has to be grown for pollination to take place.

cucumber between muslin or gauze and apply it to closed eyelids for about 15 minutes. It is not surprising that the humble cucumber is so beneficial when we consider the many vitamins and minerals it contains — providing that organic minerals are in the growing mixture in the first place, of course.

Part 9

The wonders of weeds

I REMEMBER clearly a field worker of mine from commercial days who would plant vegetables by the thousand in all weathers. She often took weeds home with her to eat and that led me to hope that their high mineral content would also benefit me. To this day, my family and I still eat nettles, dandelions and chickweed, as well as speedwell, when they are in season. Weeds have wonderful health-giving properties, especially if they grow on fertile, organic ground.

For example, speedwell. Who would have thought that such a tiny weed could shift coughs from chests so quickly? Two or three sprigs dropped into a cup of boiling water and flavoured with honey have been used to treat coughs and colds for hundreds of years, without any of the side-effects of modern drugs. And a few of the little blue Speedwell flowers scattered into the salad bowl have a well-earned reputation for stimulating the gastric juices and cleansing the blood.

But, most highly of all, I prize my nettlebeds. They never let me down. At the end of a hard winter most plots of spring greens look as if they have just about survived a gruelling boxing bout, and are useless for eating. So I turn to nettles, prepared just like spinach, they are delicious. It's easy to avoid any painful stings while gathering them by wearing rubber gloves.

And because nettles contain huge quantities of iron I never treat this weed merely as a stand-by vegetable. Nettle pie, containing cooked nettles, a mixture of mashed potato, onion and chopped hard-boiled eggs, all baked inside crisp pastry and served with grated cheese has been a favourite in country cottages for generations.

Another friendly weed is the dandelion. Its leaves are rich in vitamin A, and for me this is reason enough to value it whenever it appears. So it is a bonus to find that the dandelion cleanses the blood and is a digestive aid as well. The young leaves are

1. Rich in iron, nettles are delicious when prepared like spinach.

2. Speedwell is valuable in curing coughs and cleansing the blood.

3. Copper-rich chickweed grows well on soils which are rich in compost.

1. Dandelion can be grown from seed; this was blanched for three weeks.

2. Bistort bears lovely pink flowers in the summer months.

3. Horseradish roots take two to three years to become established.

best torn into small pieces and mixed with grated carrot, as this helps to offset the slight bitterness.

I usually upturn a dark bucket or large flower-pot over the young plant for two or three weeks.

The invasive chickweed is another weed you will always find growing around my garden. It may be unpopular as a weed, yet it contains enough copper in its leaves to propel any muscle to the finish in the London Marathon! Muscles cannot work efficiently without copper, so make sure your diet contains an adequate amount. Chickweed is free so it goes into my sandwich fillings as well as the salad bowl.

Over the years I have learnt that the best edible weeds come from organically dressed soils. They taste much better and most of them contain amazing amounts of health-giving properties.

With herbalism fast regaining its lost popularity this point is especially relevant. There are weeds and weeds and I cannot imagine health being improved by adding weeds gathered from impoverished soils to the diet. The weeds will be deficient in minerals.

Herbs to grow yourself

HERBS are useful all the year round. For instance, I would never be without herbs like thyme, bistort, salad burnet, chives and sorrel. And the time of the year when I really appreciate the hardiness of these herbs is in early spring.

No matter what the weather, I know I can always rely on salad burnet, bistort and chives to add variety to salads. The first young leaves always appear, no matter how bad the weather.

Salad burnet is a herb which fascinates me. Whenever I see new leaves pushing up it is a clear sign that spring is never far behind. I choose the new leaves for salads before they toughen with age.

With the increasing daylight, the slender shoots of the chives soon begin to appear. Bistort leaves, however, even in early spring could never be called succulent, but chopped up small and mixed into a mashed potato, I can still take advantage of the blood-cleansing and toning properties of bistort, as with the other early green herbs.

During summer the herb border flourishes. Thyme, with the rich copper content of its leaves, gives a wonderful flavour to things such as rissoles and stuffings, lifting them up to a higher plane.

Common mint is full of nutrition too, with its rich supply of potassium and manganese, and it freshens up any salad with its distinctive tangy taste.

If ever I was looking for the greatest return for my labours on the smallest area of space, I would look to my herbs. So concentrated are their properties in the small surface of their leaves and stems that a little goes a long way.

For example, parsley. It contains potassium, iron, magnesium, manganese, vitamin A and vitamin C. So, every day of the season I use one or two small sprigs for garnishing or flavouring food; I would hate to be without it.

The other annual herb which plays a big part in our household is the nasturtium. Its coloured flowers can make a salad look really interesting but the leaves are a special favourite. After eating a sandwich containing nasturtium leaves, I always get a feeling of well-being — perhaps this is due to the manganese gathered up by the leaves.

We have always had a bush of sage for flavouring food, but we were never more glad of it than when my wife had a bad attack of shingles. A drink of sage tea, night and morning, saw her through this debilitating complaint without any pain. But this shouldn't be surprising really as sage is known to be a digestion aid in the traditional sage and onion stuffing. Along with favourite herbs such as tarragon, chervil, lovage and marjoram, our winter meals become something to look forward to.

We also have a bay tree, but at the end of a very severe winter it was dying, branch by branch. For years we had opened the front door to pick off a bay leaf and used it straight

Common thyme is popular with bees as well as being highly versatile in cooking. The secret of successful growing is to cut the plant back in autumn.

away for cooking; it was particularly good in rice pudding. So when only one tiny shoot was left, the dead tree was chopped down. It was a great loss, but from that tiny shoot the tree is now as large again as ever.

I would recommend a bay tree planted in a tub for a new garden so it can be moved under cover for protection from the elements if need be.

Setting up a herb bed

ONE plant of each perennial herb is usually sufficient for a family's needs; three or four at most. The easiest way to start a border is to buy the herbs from a reputable source. Seed-raising, though a much slower method, is possible and very satisfying.

Bistort
This likes a damp position and will spread with its underground root system if left unchecked. Seed sown in early spring will produce plants by summer, which I place about two inches apart (5cm). Further plants can be grown by dividing the roots.

Chives
Seed can be sown outdoors during spring as soon as the soil is friable. As the seeds are slow to germinate, rows 12 inches (30cm) apart will allow space for hoeing. To keep stems succulent and green, a dressing of compost should be applied in the autumn. My favourite way of keeping new shoots tender is to divide the chives into a few clumps and plant in new ground each spring.

Lovage
Seed should never be sown before the soil warms up in the late spring. Choose a shady position for the seed bed and keep the soil moist until the lovage is ready for transplanting. I find that one lovage plant is more than sufficient for the needs of my family as the plant grows six feet (1.8m) tall and produces plenty of foliage. A position at the back of the herb border is vital, otherwise it can cast shade right across the herb border.

1. Pick parsley sprigs for cooking.

2. These chives are ready for pulling.

3. Bergamot red (Monarda Didyma) makes a fragrant herb tea.

Lovage leaves make a tea which is beneficial for the kidneys.

Mint

This herb can take over a border completely once it starts growing. Underground shoots will get into the tiniest of crevices, so make sure you start right. Planting mint in a barrel or bucket with no bottom is the best way to control it. Sinking it into the soil with only a fraction of the rim exposed will keep both gardener and mint happy and flourishing. It is important that the container should have no bottom to it, otherwise it can easily dry out. There are many different varieties of mint, but my favourite is garden mint or *mentha viridis.*

Herbs in general are a hardy race, but they still benefit from a regular, yearly feed. So, when planting up, I make sure there is enough space left between the plants for a good composted autumn mulch.

Nasturtium

To encourage fast germination I leave seed sowing until late spring. I choose a sunny position as this also encourages fast growth and large succulent leaves. Blackfly usually avoids nasturtiums if mature compost containing calcified seaweed is incorporated into the soil. Seaweed taken up in the leaves seems to be a great deterrent.

Parsley

The seed is often difficult to germinate, particularly if a cold snap intervenes after seed has been sown, or if the surface soil dries out. To get over this, I like to germinate seeds on damp blotting-paper which has been cut into long strips. I leave them in a warm room until the seed has chitted before placing outdoors. The seed and blotting-paper should be covered with fine soil and gently firmed. I leave 12 inches (30cm) between rows and to encourage bushy plants I always allow about eight inches (20cm) between the plants in the rows.

Sorrel

Seed sown in the spring will germinate quickly. When transplanting I allow 12 inches (30cm) between the plants and rows so there is space for the plants to produce lush, wide leaves. Sorrel leaves are much sought after in France, where bunches of leaves can be purchased in the markets; I chop them up for my salads. This is another plant which I place towards the back of the border.

Common thyme

Thyme is a large plant when fully grown. So new plants will need to be placed at least 15 inches (38cm) apart. I find that seed sown in

Salad burnet is an attractive plant with tasty, edible leaves.

early spring will produce plants large enough to set out in the herb border by the autumn. The secret of growing good fresh thyme is to cut the plant back in autumn to encourage new growth. Roots should also be divided each year to form new strong plants. Bees start working the moment thyme comes into flower and are still there until the last head fades away.

Garden sage
Sage can also be raised from seed. Sowing seeds in late spring after the frosts have finished provides plants for the autumn, but buying plants from a reputable nursery is, of course, faster. My sage plants came from a neighbour who gave me a few stems complete with heel and they all rooted easily. I keep the stock fresh in a similar way each year, by breaking off and planting stems, complete with heel, 18 inches (45cm) apart. Three years is about the maximum time I keep sage bushes before replacing them in the border.

Sage tea has many curative powers as well as flavouring for stuffing.

Part 10

These undamaged carrots were grown outdoors and dusted weekly with seaweed meal.

Coping with pests

WHEN IT comes to plagues of pests in the vegetable and fruit garden some years are worse than others. If the wind blows from the east then I'm on the look-out for green fly or black fly. And from close contact with brassica-root fly I know I can expect to see the tell-tale, ash-like eggs towards the end of April, in its favourite laying area, just at the base of brassica plants.

Then there is the carrot-root fly! This keeps to its annual routine, arriving as soon as the hedge-parsley begins to flower. But, with 30,000 miles of hedging removed in the last generation or two, much hedge-parsley has vanished, and carrot crops have become a second home to these tenacious pests.

The recent phenomenon where vast areas of land being cropped with oil-seed rape, has meant a big increase in brassica pests. As well as the hazard of a superior, immune race of carrot-root fly we are also threatened with superior, immune races of brassica pests, especially the cabbage stem flea beetle.

Over the years some tricks have been developed to thwart most of these invaders and many gardeners will go to great lengths especially to avoid using poisonous sprays.

Take, for example, that trick of fooling the cabbage-root fly with yogurt cartons. I tried it one year and was delighted to see my brassicas growing free from damage. But come clearance time and what a job I was faced with! Anybody trying to remove waxed yogurt cartons from the roots of pulled brassica plants will know what I mean. That idea was definitely discarded.

Nowadays, I plant all my brassica plants in V-trenches, and I whistle while I work, because this method always works. The pest never varies its habits: its eggs must be laid at the base of each brassica plant, down in the bottom of the trench. The eggs will hatch and the grubs will steadily feed on the brassica roots.

Only the carrots on the right were given protection.

1. The V-trench method in action. These brassica plants are growing in base of the trench, protected by *Papronet*.

2. The V-trench has been filled in with compost and levelled.

3. The plants are ready for cutting; no damage from the cabbage root fly.

But it doesn't worry me! The grubs can have that lot because new roots will emerge higher up the stem when I level off the trench with well-rotted compost. I do this about mid-May, while the grubs get busy and get their fill from the bottom roots. I make sure the ground is firmed round each plant and then that puts an end to the problem!

Masses of new healthy roots will form higher up the stem and carry my crop to fruition. It may be a week late — but it's poison-free! I have never seen any sign of grub damage in the higher root system since adopting this method, some 15 years ago.

Combatting the carrot-root fly, however, is another story. Its ancestors were no bother in years gone by. I always used to avoid carrot-root fly damage by sowing the seed after July 14, but this golden era came to an end with the arrival of the carrot barons.

Their huge, mono-cropping acreages of carrots with the attendant powerful pesticides brought forth the super carrot-root fly. These pests have turned out to be worse than the hordes of Gengis Khan who tormented Europe in the distant past! Carrots sown as late as October can still attract armies of carrot-root fly.

But, just like the mosquito, carrot-root flies haven't yet managed to crawl through porous plastic netting of the kind that lets in the rain but keeps out everything else. So when I adopted the anti-mosquito net method I was able to control this pest. It was tedious, but it worked. Erecting tents of this netting took time but the carrots growing underneath were certainly protected.

My next success proved a lot simpler. It involved dusting the carrot rows with a fine cloud of seaweed dust, on a routine weekly basis, with a hand-held dusting machine bought for this purpose. From then on my family have never wanted for carrots.

However, this is not the end of the seaweed story. For years now I have added calcified seaweed to every compost heap and liquid seaweed in every type of foliar feed, because of its natural mineral content, something that no healthy soil should be without.

But an additional spin-off showed up when neighbouring broad bean crops grown on chemicals, were both hit by black fly attacks. Mine in the middle was completely free. There is something remarkable about seaweed, and black fly and green fly just don't like it.

1. Companion planting which didn't work.
2. Look at the club root (3.). Growing by the V-trench method overcomes this problem.

Ways with comfrey

IN really bad years one needs to go in with all guns firing, and turn to comfrey for additional armoury. I remember one year when we had a long hot dry spell and green fly was spoiling the crops by the acre all round. Green fly was national news, swarming everywhere except in one place — my garden!

Even though newspapers reported that green fly and black fly must be swarming in from the Continent, they did not prosper on my patch, and the reason wasn't hard to find. It was there in my water barrel: comfrey leaves with a weight pressing on top, yielding a brown juice worth its weight in gold. Any strength seems to work, and when mixed together with liquid seaweed, proves a powerful deterrent.

When my original, small consignment of Bocking 14 comfrey roots arrived from the Henry Doubleday Research Association, it didn't amount to much sizewise. Each root measured about two inches square. But two years later those roots had swollen into large clumps.

Over the years I have greatly appreciated the two feet spacing they were given. I grow these huge plants specifically for their giant-sized leaves and this width of row made it so much easier to clear annual weeds from the soil.

The leaf harvest from each comfrey plant is quite amazing. Each harvest means cutting every single leaf back to soil level, and I can gather the leaves not once, not twice, but at least five times in any one season! The more the merrier as far as I am concerned, because not only can I use them in anti-pest sprays and in foliar feeds, but they figure largely in the major role of mulching.

This is important. By covering the ground around plants with comfrey leaves, I know that every time the ground is watered, it becomes a liquid feed of potash, phosphates and other vital nutrients. Tomatoes in particular do well with this treatment. Pests seem to find vigorous, thriving plants quite unappetizing.

Once I had two separate beds of summer cabbage quite close together. One had been cultivated organically for years while the other

1. Comfrey is cut to ground level. Note the absence of weeds in the soil.
2. Pest-free tomatoes are grown with mulched comfrey.
3. These potato trenches are lined with comfrey.
4. Comfrey mixed with peat and covered with polythene makes super compost worth its weight in gold.

was new ground with only one season of dressing. This was the patch which attracted the cabbage-white butterfly in hordes, leaving caterpillars by the dozen, while the other bed was entirely free.

But, does my garden, which has consistently been worked with organic methods and with emphasis on fertility, really need pest-control when there are no pests?

Apart, that is, from the odd unusual season when the slug population happens to outweigh the frog and toad population.

As I very much prefer a pest-free situation to one where a wide range of anti-pest equipment must be kept in stock, I never begrudge time and labour spent building up humus and replacing fertility. I also keep a watchful eye on the sources of fertility, and every autumn without fail I give a generous autumn dressing of manure to the comfrey plants after the first frost has destroyed the last leaf growth.

I try to vary the source of the top dressing every season. Chicken, horse and cow manure have all been used.

However, in unusually bad years for pests any number of the pests might start to appear but I'm ready for them with a selection of natural sprays. I like to vary these by including other bitter herbs with my pressed-out comfrey juice. Leaves of nettle, privet, tomato, wormwood and southernwood are all good basic materials that can be used against pest attacks.

Simmer a few leaves in a pint of water for ten minutes or so, and then soak for a day to obtain a potent juice. You can even mix all these together, then hurl this herbal Molotov cocktail at the pests with your spray gun.

I don't get an instant kill every time but may have to repeat the operation two or three times. Eventually, the enemy always beats a hasty retreat from my patch.

Sprays without chemicals

NEWCOMERS to organic gardening will need to resign themselves to spending two or three years in establishing the basic pest immunity which comes from a rich soil. A soil teeming with beneficial insect life and earth worms in abundance will be the first sign of achieving this, for they mark the difference between live soils and dead soils.

There are numerous pests and diseases which I never encountered which leads me to believe they must be chemically induced. In fact, soils which have become dead after introducing unnatural chemicals have no earth worms, and plants grown on such soils turn into a real pests' paradise.

It would seem that with the first introduction to chemicals, a plant will lose its

In my days of commercial growing, I used to spray liquid seaweed over brassica plants with good results.

Here's the evidence that a harmless snake, a useful predator, found my garden.

Herbal sprays protect some predators — but derris is fatal to ladybirds.

natural vigour and even with the herbal sprays I have described, will be a prey to pest attacks.

Fortunately for the organic beginner, who has not yet arrived at a pest-free soil condition, there are some insecticides on the market — which are not poisonous to us; pyrethrum and derris dust.

But they both have the same fault, as they sweep away the beneficial predators with the pest.

However, a little common sense can lessen this unwelcome side-effect, particularly with pyrethrum's effect on bees. Spraying at dusk after bees are all in the hive could help immensely in this direction for example.

When buying derris dust in liquid form make sure that no other ingredient has been included, and look out for the small print when buying pyrethrum. The chemical laboratory beavers have managed to synthesize this product under the name of *Pyrethroids* and I wouldn't touch it with a bargepole!

Another anti-pest product which can be obtained from Henry Doubleday Research Association (HDRA) is quassia chips, a bark which produces an exceptionally bitter fluid when simmered. In the days before organo-phosphorus poisons were introduced into horticulture, quassia chips was one of the main standbys.

Part 11

Successful soft fruits

EVER since the days when systemic pesticides first arrived I have been very wary of eating commercially grown soft fruits. Not everybody seems to appreciate that systemic pesticides are absorbed into every part of the fruit as well as the plant. No amount of washing will remove this.

Today, attractive piles of commercially grown soft fruits leave me unmoved, yet in my youth the way I gobbled them up must have kept whole farms in business. But to go through life without tasting the special flavour of soft fruits is unthinkable.

So, I continue to grow soft fruits, not so much from choice, but because of sheer necessity. At one time the idea of giving over any land to crops which only yielded a harvest for two or three weeks a year was abhorrent. In those days I much preferred to crop all of the garden with vegetables and then buy in everything else which demanded more space and maintenance. But that option is no longer open, given the widespread use of pesticides by today's fruit growers.

Soft fruits rank high in my priority list of the crops I must grow. What is summer without a bowlful of strawberries topped with cream, a blackcurrant tart or the special smell of raspberries that melt in the mouth? Such pleasures are doubled by the knowledge that soft fruits not only smell tantalizing, but they contain so much goodness as well. How can eyesight fail to benefit when soft fruits are such a good source of vitamin A? And skin and blood will surely reap the benefit of vitamin C which abounds in soft fruits picked fresh from the garden. And there is even some vitamin B to be had.

However, crops that occupy the same site year after year need special attention. I remember learning this particular aspect of soft fruit growing the hard way. My soft fruit cage was purposely sited in a convenient position, but when it was put to the test, excessive rainfall proved decisively that it was the wrong site. Raspberries and gooseberries in particular just didn't like having their roots immersed in water for months on end.

My next soft fruit area didn't suffer from the

Stages for growing super strawberries: 1. Plant runners in August or September on well composted soil laced with seaweed.

2. Flowers are pinched out to give new runners maximum growth so that they will yield a bumper crop the following year.

3. In the second year runners are allowed to fruit under protective netting, bedded with straw.

4. Cambridge Vigour growing last summer and living up to its name.

5. The straw is cleaned and tops are shaved with the lawn mower with the blades set high.

6. The area around each strawberry plant is cleaned and weeded.

7. New growth is shooting out of crowns which were hardly visible four weeks earlier and the scene is set for a good harvest.

Strawberries at their mouthwatering best.

handicap of poor drainage but then I left nothing to chance! The answer was to construct trenches 12 inches (30cm) deep and wide. I made doubly sure of good drainage by placing large stones at the bottom of the trench. Once bitten twice shy! I then covered the stones with wads of newspaper at least 12 newspapers thick. Worms live happily in wet decaying newspapers — a tip that fishermen ought to know.

As an extra inducement to the roots of soft fruit bushes I covered the newspapers with piles of compost and added bonemeal, before returning the soil to fill up the trenches again. This will last for years once the bonemeal becomes incorporated into the sub-soil.

This may sound like hard work but many runner bean growers carry out such a task every year although it's not a bean-growing technique which I use. I restrict trenching to initial preparations when I know a perennial crop is going to demand nourishment continuously from the same site. The real successes of fruit-growing lie underneath the top soil and depend too on the sub-soil being well-drained.

Like vegetables, my soft fruits are never deprived of their yearly quota of minerals. I apply seaweed meal as well as calcified seaweed to the top soil once the area has had its autumn clean-up. Soft fruits appreciate this treatment by yielding their best possible flavour. What more could anyone ask? Two ounces (50g) each of calcified seaweed and seaweed meal to the square yard (m²) around each bush is adequate but more generous dressings will help build resistance against pests.

Covering the top of this seaweed dressing is the all-important mulch of compost which I apply around the soft fruits every autumn. Weeding is easy once this area becomes friable through repeated yearly dressings.

Leaving enough space between bushes for their wide-spreading top growth results in large areas of ground where weeds can run wild. I overcome this by placing sheets of newspaper covered with grass cuttings between soft fruit rows to act as a weed barrier.

Setting the soft fruits too close together can become a problem in later years. It's amazing the way they thicken as the years roll by. Newcomers into soft fruit growing have the advantage that they can start right, because mistakes in close planting can never be rectified.

Strawberry secrets

WITH the farmer beaming from ear to ear, I remember being one of a party of toddlers told to gorge ourselves after being turned loose in a field of ripe strawberries. My grandchildren do the same. Faced with ripe strawberries how can they resist picking them? Of course I don't mind just as long as they replace the protective net. But to satisfy such a keen demand I keep my strawberry patch moving around the vegetable garden by

planting up a fresh strawberry bed each year.

To keep my strawberry patch free from disease I have an unbreakable rule. I do not allow newly planted strawberry plants to fruit in the first season, so the new runners become strong. This means pinching out all the flowers as soon as they appear. But it is well worth doing. These are the plants which are going to produce my runners. This happens annually. New runners from non-fruiting plants are left to fruit the following year and for a further three years before being scrapped.

Lashings of calcified seaweed and seaweed meal spread over the soil before setting out the new runners also help to keep disease at bay. No half measures here. For a crop which will remain on the same site for at least four years, no less than 1lb of each ingredient is applied to the square yard. Unlike

In this test planting Cambridge Vigour, in the centre, came out top.

Note the protective netting around these strawberries in their frame.

Every scrap of foliage should be shaved off and composted.

the other soft fruits, strawberries are fitted around the vegetables in my organic garden. They are fed with masses of garden compost in the three or four years they occupy their cropping area. Apart from compost, an ounce of *Back-to-Nature* to the square yard is all they receive.

Another feature of my strawberry-growing is the 'all-off' shave which I give the strawberry patch after they have finished fruiting. With the rotary lawn mower set at its highest level, I simply mow the whole area clean. Nothing is left except the visible crown, which will produce next year's growth. Cleaning up the strawberry patch until all the weeds and strawberry foliage have gone, is relatively simple. Within four weeks the area is unrecognizable, clean soil and new growth both achieved without one drop of obnoxious herbicide. In recent years I have returned strawberry waste to strawberries after composting, but this is only possible with disease-free debris.

Everybody tells me that Cambridge Vigour is breaking down with virus. Well my Cambridge Vigour is still cropping well, after ten years' service. This year Totem has joined my organic garden. From the description given by Dobies I am looking forward to enjoying them for many years.

For outdoor cropping I space my plants 30 inches (76cm) apart in the rows and 12 inches (30cm) from plant to plant. For early cropping in frames they are set 12 inches (30cm) apart each way. With this tight spacing I make a point of carefully stripping the leaf when the fruit forms to allow plenty of air to circulate and so ward off any enemies like botrytis.

Caring for currants

BLACKCURRANTS grow like crazy once they get the feel of accumulated top humus. A few blackcurrant and redcurrant bushes can really keep a family in style, so not many of each are needed. This is just as well because I allow six foot (1.8m) spacing between the rows and within the rows I leave spacing of five foot (1.5m). Setting soft fruits too close together only results in aggravation in later years.

Choosing the right variety of blackcurrants

Laxton No. 1 is my choice for ravishingly rich redcurrants.

This bush was allowed to grow wild, without a mulch but the crop was bitter and pippy.

can always be solved by planting Wellington XXX as the first choice and then any other variety that appeals. Ben Lomond and Tenah will also produce satisfying crops.

Pruning newly planted blackcurrant bushes could cause the heart to miss a beat or two, because all growth must be cut down to within two inches or so of soil level. This action allows the blackcurrant to bush out and produce plenty of stems for fruiting the following year. Keeping the bush in production means pruning out dead wood and encouraging fresh growth to come up from the base.

REDCURRANTS look dazzling when the clusters ripen into glowing red berries. My Laxton No. 1 looks as if it will go on for ever. The pruning of redcurrants is carried out somewhat differently from blackcurrants and

My crop of Delight raspberries after two dry winters, but look at the deterioration (right) after two wet winters.

Malling Promise raspberries, untainted by chemicals.

Zeva raspberries are dwarf but prolific.

many a producer and grower has supplied intricate details of this. But I find that it is really a question of cutting new lateral shoots back to the fruit buds which form at the base. The leading shoots are also shortened to eliminate surplus growth which will bear no fruit. My bush has been yielding masses of redcurrants for the whole family with the minimum of pruning.

Blowing raspberries!

RASPBERRY canes look pitifully thin when they arrive from the growers. Yet I plant them no closer than 18 inches (45cm) apart. Cutting them back to only nine inches (23cm) tall looks like butchery, but this has to be done to encourage fresh growth, which in time will yield a forest of fresh cane growth.

I bang in the supporting stakes at the same time, ready to sling supporting wires across. End posts seem to have a knack of leaning inwards once the crop gains weight, so I use additional end wedges to prevent this happening. From then onwards my basic yearly routine at the end of the fruiting season is to cut away every bit of old growth. Then I turn my attention to the new canes left growing there. I leave only the best and then no more than eight, and tie them back to the supporting wires in fan fashion.

Lots of new varieties are being developed with many only available from specialist

Loganberries are grown in the same way as raspberries. These produced a mass of flowers (top) but the crop's flavour was disappointing. They were the wrong variety for my soil.

companies. Delight and Malling Admiral are two new varieties that are worth growing. Different varieties react differently to weather conditions. By mixing varieties along the same row, I hope that if the season starts playing havoc, then at least one variety ought to come up trumps.

Part 12

Hardware that helps out

MANY YEARS ago on holiday in West Germany I remember feeling appalled at the limited number of tools used by smallholders there, and at how primitive they were too. Back home, my hydraulic equipment did away with the need for physical exertion and would have made short work of some of those jobs. But recent visits to that same country showed me a different story: every holding is a model of efficiency, tools for every conceivable job are neatly stored and ready for instant use. This really is the best way for any garden to be. And what a range of good equipment there is.

Take, for example, the new swing-back hoes recently introduced by *Clavering.* Ever since they were launched I have used the seven-inch as well as the nine-inch model in my own garden. It has solved the vexing problem of cut weeds that simply root again, for this new, swing-back hoe not only severs the weeds but tears them to pieces on the back swing. When used on a sunny day they make short work of the most stubborn of weeds. They save time, and even if they seem expensive, they are still a very good buy.

And so is the Lincolnshire longhorn hoe. When I first came across it in the depths of Lincolnshire I was immediately impressed with its ability to glide over large areas of ground. The cutting edge measures 18 inches (45cm) and a forward motion soon cleans up really weedy ground. I have used it in my garden for some years now, and I was delighted to see that the Henry Doubleday Research Association had become distributors. Compared

Above: The time-saving swing-back hoe is demonstrated by Nigel Clavering.

Right: The Lincolnshire longhorn hoe has been used for the past 100 years.

with the pressed-out tin tools one sees, the Lincolnshire longhorn hoe is well made and is an asset to any garden.

A swing-back hoe and the Lincolnshire longhorn hoe take care of those garden weeds which are always ready to take advantage, such as when bad weather prevents me getting a thick top mulch down in time, or when I manage to take a couple of weeks' holiday or, unkindest cut of all, when weed seeds blow in from nearby fields.

Close work around individual plants calls for extra care and a three-inch (8cm) short-handled swan-neck hoe is specially designed for this task, although this isn't the only job I use it for. The angle of the blade is excellent

This wheelbarrow is well designed because its legs are spaced well apart for comfortable pushing.

Provided the blade is set at its highest setting the rotary lawn mower makes short work of weedy areas.

This Mountfield rotary digger makes soil preparation an easy task for the organic gardener.

for drawing out shallow drills for seed sowing by following along the slight indent which I have made by treading along my garden-line.

Machines make light work

A MACHINE which is important in my garden is the *Mountfield* rotary lawn mower. At one time my lawn was an anxiety, not because of weedkillers or chemicals contaminating the surface — it was always safe for children to play on — but because I found the cuttings hard to handle. The change came when I discovered that the bruising action of the rotary blades instantly released grass juices and turned the difficult material into a valuable compost activator.

It can be a problem to keep grass growing in some gardens, but there is a good way to solve it. After cutting and removing grass week after week, something in return is needed, at least once a year. This is where the grass scarifier comes into its own, because I want grass, not moss. When I think back to the aching muscles and blisters of the days when moss raking was carried out by hand, it causes a shudder.

The new *AL-KO* electric lawn scarifier is wonderful. Once up and down the garden is all that is needed to tear moss and weeds out of the lawn and grasses respond joyfully once they spread and grow. What a life-saver such a machine becomes when other jobs are pressing for attention! A regular dressing of seaweed minerals can still be applied to the lawn by hand without much bother as the sort of distributor which will handle this job has not yet come my way.

1. Chopping thick brassica stems for the compost heap is a laborious task.

2. Dusting with protective seaweed powder is easy with this hand-propelled duster.

3. The shredder completes the task of breaking down bulky waste in seconds.

4. The finished compost — but damp conditions in the autumn can produce disastrous results.

One machine I hesitate to recommend is my *AL-KO* compost shredder. The idea of shredding garden weeds has terrific appeal and when I used my machine during the summer with fibrous dry materials, everything was perfect. A pre-mix of wet and dry materials produces a beautifully shredded compost, which when used as a mulch between growing crops, resulted in beautifully healthy vegetables. Unfortunately, when dry materials were no longer available in the autumn, my output dropped to zero. The sad fact is that the shredding machine only works with dry materials. Hedge clippings and woody materials are dry enough for shredding at any time of year.

It is a tremendous boon when all the mineral-rich vegetation is returned to the soil. Also, it removes any excuse for that bane of my life, those obnoxious, harmful, smelly bonfires. So I wouldn't be without my shredder even when its use is restricted.

Gadgets for the home gardener

BESIDES machinery, every organic gardener needs a good selection of gardening aids to lighten the work load. I have bought various wheelbarrows in my time and with some I have lived to rue the day, like the one designed with straight leg supports that are so placed they gouge my own legs whenever the wheelbarrow is being pushed along.

I much prefer a model made from endless tubular metal and the legs cleverly splayed to give plenty of walking space. Plastic 'ball' wheelbarrows look attractive and easy to push but they suffer from the drawback of a wheel too wide to

1. The *Ambig Seed-Raiser:* small enough to stand on a sunny windowsill.

2. Purpose-built compost bins are ideal for the organic garden. Here is the *Rotol* compost converter (foreground) with the Compostabin.

3. Parts of my garden look like a major production line as piles of compost are left to mature under black polythene.

All lined up; these bins are full of kitchen waste rotting down into excellent worm compost.

use between crops.

Over the years my holding has been littered with broken spade handles and the cause of the problem has always been the same: that point where the handle joins on to the spade. My best purchase is the type which has a continuous metal support right up to the spade handle.

I have used the *Ambig Seed-Raiser* ever since it was launched. Not only does it allow me to raise all my early vegetable seeds on the window ledge, but it also looks good. The secret of the *Ambig Seed-Raiser,* is of course its capilliary wick which is a great disease-resisting aid. With the leaves kept dry, mildew and botrytis are kept well under control.

The polystyrene *A & D* seed trays are also a great aid in potting-on all the seedlings. The polystyrene used is a good insulating material and therefore does two things: It prevents the potting compost from drying out and keeps the compost much warmer.

Plastic water butts are ideal for extracting health-promoting juice for foliar feeding. An equal quantity of comfrey and nettle leaves produces concentrated liquid food which puts the chemical alternative into the shade. Pressing out the juice with a weight placed on top of the leaves will get over the problem of flies and smells associated with making liquid manure with water. The concentrated

liquid keeps well and when diluted can be sprayed onto all vegetable, flower and fruit crops.

The type of sprayer used for this purpose depends on the size of the garden. There are many plastic sprayers available and it is really a question of size versus time, the larger model needing less time for constant refilling. But then, the larger the sprayer, the more weight to contend with when carrying the contents around. I find that the weight of my three and a half-gallon (16l) Hills knapsack sprayer is not very popular with the ladies and this factor should be borne in mind.

The gardening aid for which I feel great affection is the small hand-propelled duster. Since I bought this handy machine to apply a weekly dusting of seaweed powder to my carrot crop, the carrot-fly has ceased to be such an enemy.

As time goes by, black polythene sheeting covers larger and larger areas of my garden and I find that sheets cut to fit my 30 feet by 12 feet (9×3.6m) plots are easiest to manage. Prices vary according to the thickness of the material. For all my over-wintered mulches I have settled on the 500 gauge thickness. Use small plastic bags filled with stones to keep the sheets from blowing away.

Cardboard is made from wood and is a valuable raw material. I keep bundles of cardboard tied up and stacked ready for the autumn mulching. It is worth keeping the bundles dry with a polythene wrap as it makes the job of spreading the cardboard that much easier.

I never get very far in the garden without discovering the need for at least one plastic bucket, bought in any High Street. I use them all the time, but the greatest use is as a quantity measure, when I'm making up mixes by ratio as well as spreading the mixes according to area of ground.

The compostabin is ideal if you are turning the compost heap after its first couple of weeks. By lifting the bin up and off altogether, the heap can easily be forked over to let air into every part. This aeration speeds up the rotting process, particularly of the weed seeds. And I know when I replace the compostabin back over the heap again that it is keeping in the heat and keeping out the wind and the wet.

Some time ago I evolved a system of turning domestic waste into plant food with the help of plastic dustbins and manure worms, but garden waste with its weed seeds is never used in this domestic system which is fully described in my booklet, *Worm Compost*.

To put together an organic garden is not a quick job, yet once the system gets into its stride the results are truly satisfying. I try hard to make sure that everything is in place and take stock every autumn to ensure everything will be there when I want it — even labels and marking pens. Gardening time is too valuable to waste in chasing after essential items! Happy Gardening!

Further Information

Part 4
Reskia lettuce from J. W. Boyce, 67 Station Road, Sotham, Ely, Cambridgeshire.

Part 6
Working with the Stars available from Lanthorn Press, Pesedar, East Grinstead, Sussex.

Part 10
In the event of difficulty in purchasing any of these products then the Henry Doubleday Research Association (HDRA) have a small mail order service. HDRA, Convent Lane, Bocking, Braintree, Essex. Tel: Braintree (0376) 24083.

Part 11
Landspeed is available from Hofels direct mail order service. 20lb Landspeed costs £5.99 plus £2 for delivery. Write to Hofels Pure Foods Ltd, Stowmarket Road, Woolpit, Bury St Edmunds, Suffolk IP30 9QS.

Back-To-Nature is made by Britannia Industries and is available from most garden centres, £1.42 (1kg) and £4.76 (5kg).

Part 12
For garden sprayers: Hills Industries Ltd, Pontygwindy Industrial Estate, Caerphilly, Mid-Glamorgan CF8 1XF.

Compostabin: Garrotta Products Ltd, Station Mills, Bute Street, Luton, Beds.

Rotol bin: Lindvale Plastics, Waverley Street, Coatbridge, Lanarkshire.

Mountfield Rotary Mower: For nearest stockists write to: G. D. Mountfield Ltd, Reform Road, Maidenhead, Berks.

The Kiobitz Hand Duster: J. Gibbs Ltd., Ripley, Surrey.

Black Plastic Sheeting: Greenfield Plastics Ltd, Laitwood, Burton Street, Brixham, Devon TQ5 9JA.

Clavering Organic Real Gardening Ltd, 5 Chaucer Industrial Estate, Ditton's Road, Polegate, East Sussex.

Swing-back hoe: Suffolk Herbs, Sawyers Farm, Little Carnard, Sudbury, Suffolk CO10 0NY.

Lincolnshire Longhorn hoe: Palmer and Shelley Ltd, Nechells Place, Birmingham B7 5AC.

AL-KO: 1 Industrial Estate, Medomslay Road, Consett, County Durham.

Ambig Seed-Raiser: Unit 18, Goldsworth Park, Woking, Surrey.

A & D Seed-Raisers and plastic butts from garden centres.

Worm Compost: 80p from The Soil Association, Walnut Tree Manor, Haughley, Stowmarket, Suffolk.

Index

Other recommended reading . . .

A MONTH BY MONTH GUIDE
TO ORGANIC GARDENING

Lawrence D Hills. A step-by-step and month-by-month guide to growing healthy, tasty fruit and vegetables using natures own resources to build a fertile, pest and disease resistant soil. Chapters for each month include information on planting, sowing, pruning and the full organic routine for fruit and vegetables. The author, who has pioneered organic gardening world-wide and is Founder and Director of the Henry Doubleday Research Association, explains the nutritive value of garden crops and includes advice for the many allergy victims who have to grow their own food organically.

THE UNHEATED GREENHOUSE

HOW TO MAXIMIZE ITS POTENTIAL

Ronald H Menage. *Illustrated.* With soaring fuel costs, even maintaining minimum temperatures in a greenhouse has become an expensive operation for gardeners. Author explains the many advantages of an unheated greenhouse and how to operate it for maximum benefit. Equipping and maintenance, and care of plants, is fully covered in connection with cold greenhouse culture. Almost anything grown outdoors can be grown in an unheated greenhouse. Soil is not essential, pot growth often giving better results, so the greenhouse, like its heated counterpart, can be erected on concrete, in a paved yard, or even on a flat roof or large balcony. *Contents include:* Siting and erecting the greenhouse; Fitting out the greenhouse; Making the most of free sun heat and conservation; Putting the unheated greenhouse to practical use and routine maintenance; Growing plants from seed; Fruit and vegetables; Pot plants and flowers for cutting; Shrubs, perennials and climbers; Plants from bulbs.

DISCOVER THE SECRETS OF 'COMPANION PLANTING'

Gertrud Franck. Did you know that some plants thrive together and some are incompatible? That culinary herbs actually stimulate the growth of other crops? The author shows how to get the best from your garden by copying nature, where plants and crops flourish, without the aid of human intervention, simply by means of compatibility. This method requires no artificial substances costing money and time, but relies entirely upon making the best use of the natural interaction of organic matter for composting, fertilization, pest control and preserving garden produce. Includes advice on how to avoid heavy digging and to achieve not only peak production, but also a garden that remains disease and pest free.